In Memory of
My "Nana",
Lela Mae Harrison

Your faith and belief gave me the courage to live
this dream. Hopefully, I made you proud!

IF IT DOES NOT FIT, MUST YOU ACQUIT?
Your Humorous Guide to the Law
by Sean Carter

Published by:
Lawpsided Press, Inc.
P.O. Box 1867
Chino Hills, CA 91709
Phone: (909) 393-1884
Fax: (909) 393-0922
http://www.lawpsided.com
bookinfo@lawpsided.com

International Standard Book Number: 0-9723136-0-5
Library of Congress Control Number: 2002110577

Printed in the United States of America

THIS BOOK CONTAINS THE OPINIONS AND IDEAS OF THE AUTHOR. IT IS INTENDED TO PROVIDE HELPFUL AND INFORMATIVE MATERIAL ON THE LAW. IT IS SOLD WITH THE UNDERSTANDING THAT THE AUTHOR AND PUBLISHER ARE <u>NOT</u> RENDERING LEGAL ADVICE IN THIS BOOK. IF YOU REQUIRE PERSONAL ASSISTANCE OR ADVICE, PLEASE CONSULT A COMPETENT PROFESSIONAL.

THE AUTHOR AND PUBLISHER HAVE USED THEIR BEST EFFORTS IN PREPARING THIS BOOK. NEVERTHELESS, THE AUTHOR AND THE PUBLISHER DO NOT WARRANT THE ACCURACY AND COMPLETENESS OF ALL INFORMATION CONTAINED HEREIN. FURTHERMORE, THE AUTHOR AND PUBLISHER SPECIFICALLY DISCLAIM ANY RESPONSIBILITY FOR ANY LIABILITY, LOSS OR RISK, PERSONAL OR OTHERWISE, WHICH IS INCURRED AS A CONSEQUENCE, DIRECTLY OR INDIRECTLY, OF THE USE AND APPLICATION OF ANY OF THE CONTENTS OF THIS BOOK.

ACKNOWLEDGMENTS

This book could not have been written without the support of many people.

First and foremost, to my wife and two sons, thank you for your patience and support during this project. I have not taken for granted your willingness to allow me the time to "live my making."

To the people of Lawpsided Press, I can honestly say that I have never enjoyed working with *anyone* so much. Without your help, this book would still be in the back of a closet somewhere.

To my illustrator and cover designer, Sharon Stockdale, we did it! You agreed to work with a complete stranger under very trying deadlines. You put your heart and soul into this book and I will be forever grateful.

To my editors, Lee Spalding, Pat Windolph and Scott Flanders, I could not have found better editors to work on this project. In particular, I want to thank you Lee for being more of a friend to me than you'll ever know. You provided my start as a columnist and have been there for every step of this journey. Thank you! Likewise, Scott, your friendship and talent have made this book (and me) immeasurably better.

In addition, I thank all of the family members and friends who provided an ear to talk to and a shoulder to cry on during this odyssey. I can't thank you enough. This is particularly true of my parents, Arthur and Charlotte Carter. Thank you for everything! Also, to my good friend and fellow author, Stephen Burke, thank you for allowing me to borrow your vision with your first book, *Surrender*.

Lastly, I would like to thank some people whom I've never met. Yet, their words of encouragement and support have helped me to "water this bamboo tree." Thank you Les Brown and T.D. Jakes. Time and time again, I have turned to your words of wisdom for comfort, inspiration and courage.

If It Does Not Fit, Must You Acquit?

YOUR HUMOROUS GUIDE TO THE LAW

Table of Contents

Table of Contents

WHAT'S IN THIS BOOK

Do you know the difference between *caveat emptor* and an empty bowl of caviar? Likewise, if you've been carjacked, are you the victim of a robbery, burglary, or are you just happy to finally be rid of that 1983 Chevy Nova?

In *If It Does Not Fit, Must You Acquit?*, you will find the answer to these questions and hundreds of equally silly questions. More importantly, you will learn the fundamental principles of our legal system.

The book is broken into six major parts:

- **Constitutional Law**
- **Contracts**
- **Torts (Personal Injury)**
- **Real Property**
- **Criminal Law**
- **Courtroom Law**

Each part is further broken into chapters. Each chapter discusses related principles of that area of the law and ends with a light-hearted quiz designed to reinforce the major lessons of the chapter.

Of course, at this point,

many of you are asking, "Why would I want to learn about the law?" Well, the answer is simple – because you've already paid for the book and there is no return policy.

Seriously, understanding the law is important because it pervades every aspect of American life. The law touches every relationship you form (husband-wife, employer-employee, used car salesman-sucker, etc.). Also, it governs everything you own (houses, cars, stocks, Beanie Baby collections, etc.).

In short, the law is as pervasive as Internet porn, only less vital to the economy. And sadly, ignorance of the law is not an excuse. Therefore, it only makes sense to acquire a basic understanding of your rights and obligations under the law.

Now, of course, I understand that a book on the law can be as boring as an Al Gore speech on global warming, nuclear peace treaties or any subject for that matter. Therefore, this book is peppered with jokes, cartoons, side-bars and snippets from my weekly legal humor column in an effort to compensate for its subject matter.

In fact, the publisher of this book, Lawpsided Press, makes the following guarantee:

The time you spend reading this book will be the most enjoyable time of your life; provided that:

(1) Up until now, you've had a *very* boring life; and

(2) You get hit by a bus shortly after finishing this book.

WHAT'S NOT IN THIS BOOK

Before reading any further, I want to make clear that this book is <u>not</u> a do-it-yourself guide to the law. This book will not teach you how to write a will, form a corporation or commit a double murder in Brentwood and get away with it.

The purpose of this book is to give you a basic understanding of the law. This basic understanding is meant to serve you in your daily interactions. However, it is not intended to make you into the next F. Lee Bailey (or even, Beetle Bailey for that matter).

Every lawyer must go through the same three-step process – college, law school and frontal lobotomy (although not necessarily in that order). And as you can see from the actions of Congress, the Supreme Court and the "Dream Team," there are *no* exceptions to this rule.

Furthermore, as you will see in these pages, the law is *extremely* complex. Moreover, the laws differ in each state and the federal government has its own set of laws.

Even worse, each law is subject to a number of exceptions. And those exceptions have exceptions, which have exceptions and so on.

For instance, in the English language, we have a rule that states, "*i* before *e* except after *c*." In the law, this same rule would be:

"*i* before *e* except after *c*, unless *c* is preceded by any consonant but *p* or *q* and except when appearing in a word that is either at or near the beginning of a sentence, except when that sentence is the first or fourth sentence of a paragraph, unless that paragraph is the first paragraph on an even-numbered page."

Obviously, a book covering this level of detail would be as large as several telephone directories, only far less interesting to read. Therefore, whenever possible, I have simplified legal rules to reflect the outcome in *most* cases.

Needless to say, your particular situation may

not fit into the majority case. Therefore, I *strongly* urge you to seek assistance, when necessary, from a competent attorney (i.e., not me).

Besides, any do-it-yourself program is likely to turn into a pay-more-for-someone-to-do-it-right-later program. For instance, recently, my wife and I got the "bright" idea of repairing our thermostat. After all, we have 11 years of post-high school education between us. Surely, we can fix a thermostat, right?

Of course, we could not have been more wrong if we were Dan Quayle in the final round on *Jeopardy*. Two blown fuses and $600 later, we learned that, although a degree in French may have some uses (although we haven't found one yet), it's always better to rely on professionals.

Finally, I would like to point out that you *might* be offended by some of the humor in this book. Actually, who am I kidding? You *will* be offended by some of the humor in this book. This is not because the humor is vulgar or in bad taste (well, except for that joke on page 28) but rather because I make fun of almost everyone. In fact, on the next page, you find a partial list of "victims."

Therefore, I ask for your patience and understanding while reading this book. When you encounter a joke that's not funny (i.e., it's about your favorite entertainer, politician or worse, you), please continue reading. In no time, you will find a joke that is funny (i.e., it's about your in-laws). Remember, he who laughs last isn't related to anyone on the last page of this book.

─────────── Disclaimers ───────────

Joke Subject List

Marv Albert	Idaho	Philip Morris
Amusement parks	Illegal immigrants	Postal employees
Amway	In-laws	Elvis Presley
Pamela Anderson	Internet dating	Prince
Backstreet Boys	Magic Johnson	Process servers
Scott Baio	Judge Joe Brown	Public schools
Robert Blake	Judge Wapner	Dan Quayle
The Brady Bunch	Julio Iglesias	Ronald Reagan
The British	Juries	Rob Reiner
James Brown	Ted Kennedy	Mary Lou Retton
Pat Buchanon	Jack Kervorkian	Dennis Rodman
Anheiser Bush	Don King	O.J. Simpson
George W. Bush	Larry King	Spouses
California	Kool & The Gang	Jerry Springer
Car dealers	Ricki Lake	Starbucks
Johnny Carson	Landlords	Howard Stern
Dick Clark	Lawyers	Martha Stewart
Bill Clinton	Monica Lewinski	Oliver Stone
Andrew Dice Clay	Carl Lewis	Darryl Strawberry
Cindy Crawford	Jerry Lewis	Supreme Court
Children	Rush Limbaugh	Tennessee
Congress	Jennifer Lopez	John Tesh
Bob Dole	Madonna	Texaco
Denny's	Maine	The Three Stooges
Clint Eastwood	Marriage	Strom Thurmond
Eminem	Massachusetts	Linda Tripp
Enron Executives	M.C. Hammer	Truckers
Exxon	Montana	Donald Trump
Flavored coffees	N'Sync	Mike Tyson
The Flinstones	NRA	The United Way
Jane Fonda	New York	Vampires
The French	Oklahoma	Wal-Mart
Mark Fuhrman	Shaquille O'Neal	Washington
Zsa Zsa Gabor	New Jersey	Stevie Wonder
Bill Gates	Parents	Tiger Woods
Goldilocks	Ru Paul	WorldCom
Al Gore	Pennsylvania	WWF
Hugh Grant	Ross Perot	Wyoming
HOAs	Tom Petty	**YOU**

CONTRACTS

LIKE BONDAGE, JUST NOT AS FUN

CONTRACTS
OVERVIEW

Each of us enters into hundreds of contracts in a lifetime. In fact, I think it was Descartes who said, "I contract, therefore I am." Or maybe, it was Donald Trump. In any event, contracts come in all shapes and sizes -- some good (your home mortgage), some bad (that never used health club membership) and some ugly (marriage). Therefore, it makes sense to have a basic understanding of them.

In fact, if you choose to pay attention to anything in this book (which is highly unlikely), then make sure you pay attention to what's written in this section. Your knowledge of how to make contracts and more importantly, how to break them, could be worth *millions*.

In this section, we will discuss how to form a valid contract. Remember, without a valid contract, your rights are about as meaningful as the lyrics to a Kool & The Gang song ("Celebrate good times, come on!"). We will also discuss some of the ways to get out of a contract. After all, entering a contract is much like putting on a girdle; it is sometimes a struggle to get into but it's *always* a relief to get out of it. Lastly, we will discuss the consequences for not living up to your obligations under a contract (i.e., who can sue you and for how much?).

Chapter 1

FORMATION OF A CONTRACT
You Agreed To What?!

There are four essential elements to a contract:

(1) an offer;

(2) an acceptance;

(3) consideration; and

(4) a lawsuit.

Actually, although the fourth element isn't strictly required, it does seem to be a standard part of any 21st century contract.

As for the first three elements, they are required. Only after *all* of these elements are present is there a binding contract. Not that it really matters because, as you will see, the law often requires a person to act even without a valid contract.

THE OFFER

An offer is a communication made with the *present intention* to enter into an agreement. For instance, let's suppose you say to your mother, "When I get really rich, I'm going to buy you a home." This statement is not an offer and will not obligate you to buy her a home if you ever become really rich.

In addition, the person making the offer must intend to make a contract. You can't enforce a contract simply because someone says something that sounds like an offer but really isn't one. For instance, if I say to you, "I'm so hungry, I'd give my left arm for a pizza," you can't call Dominos and start warming up your power saw. Obviously, I didn't really mean to trade my arm for a pizza. However, if you throw in some of those chicken wings, you might have a deal.

Also, the offer must describe the agreement in meaningful detail. For example, let's suppose Homeless Harry is standing on the side of the road holding up a sign that reads: "Will Work for Food". In this case, you can't stop your car and yell, "I accept!" and then make Harry paint your entire house for a Twinkie.

On the other hand, the offer need not be described

in so much detail that it gives you a headache either. The offer simply must communicate the basic terms of the deal. Therefore, if Homeless Harry has a sign that reads: "Will Smear This Filthy Rag Across Your Windshield in Exchange for the Loose Change in Your Ashtray," this is a valid offer.

Finally, the person making the offer (the *offeror*) may withdraw the offer at any time *before* acceptance. Small children seem to have an instinctual knowledge of this principle. As a result, one child will often say to another child, "Want some of my candy?" And before the other child can respond, the first child will yell, "Psych!" That's because kids know that before the offer has been accepted, it can be withdrawn at any time.

However, there is an exception to this rule in the case of an option. For example, most car leases come with the option to buy the car at the end of the term. When you return to the dealership at the end of the lease, the dealer can't use the "Psych!" defense to keep you from buying the

car. However, he can use some of those same tricks that made you lease that lime green Yugo in the first place.

THE ACCEPTANCE

An offer can be accepted in many ways. For one, an offer can be accepted verbally. And there are no magic words that must be used, such "I accept" or "I do." For example, the conversation below is a perfectly valid offer and acceptance:

Jeb: Wanna split a six-pack?

Zeke: You betcha!

Acceptance can also be *inferred* from action. Therefore, Zeke could have *silently* accepted Jeb's offer by simply buying a six-pack of Red Neck Lager. In this case, Jeb would be obligated to sell his Dukes of Hazzard trading card set to pay for his half of the six-pack.

However, as a general rule, and contrary to common belief, silence is <u>not</u> acceptance. Therefore, a merchant can't send you a truckload of Spam with the following note:

Dear Spam Lover:

Because we know that you appreciate the wonderful taste of high quality meat-*like* products, we have decided to send you a 30-year supply of Spam (no refrigeration necessary). If you do not wish to accept and pay the low price of $42,000 for this nutritious product, please say the following to the two large, angry-looking delivery drivers: "Hey, Boneheads! Take this Spam and stick it up your #$%^!" Otherwise, we will consider your silence to be acceptance. Tiny and Bruiser will return for payment in full on Tuesday.

In this case, you would have to be a masochist to formally "reject" this offer. However, your understandable silence in this situation will not be considered acceptance of the offer.

In fact, as a matter of federal law, if a merchant sends you a product that you didn't request, you may keep it without paying for it. Of course, I have no

idea what you would do with 2,700 pounds of simulated meat product. And I really don't want to know either.

Interesting problems sometimes arise over the timing of the acceptance. For instance, let's suppose Hayseed Harry goes away to college. However, he soon becomes homesick for his best gal, Daisy Mae. One

lonely night, he writes her a letter proposing marriage (the offer). Daisy Mae and the "kinfolk" are delighted when the letter is read to them by a literate passerby.

Two days later, Daisy writes and mails her enthusiastic acceptance, which consists of one word, "Okee!" That same night,

Harry meets Christie Coed at a frat party and decides that he is too young to be married. The next morning, he calls Daisy Mae to revoke his offer of marriage. Two days later, Daisy Mae's acceptance arrives in the mail.

The question in this scenario is whether Harry took back his offer of marriage before Daisy Mae accepted. Believe it or not, in most states, Daisy Mae accepted the offer upon *mailing* the letter. This is the so-called "mailbox rule." As a result, Harry's withdrawal was ineffective because it was made *after* Daisy Mae's acceptance.

Generally, the mailbox rule applies to all offers unless the offeror requires a specific method of acceptance. For instance, let's suppose two guys, Pathetic Pete and Pitiful Paul, are arguing about who would be better in bed – Samantha from *Bewitched* or Jeannie from *I Dream of Jeannie* (yes, guys argue about this type of thing *all of the time*). After hours of debate, Pete says, "Let's ask John what he thinks. I bet you $20 that he agrees with me." If Pete is like most guys, Paul can only accept this "offer" by shaking hands.

Similar timing issues arise when the offer is rejected. However, in this case, the "mailbox rule" works in reverse. A rejection is not effective until received.

For instance, let's suppose Daisy Mae decides that her third cousin, Arnold, would make a better husband. Therefore, on the day after receiving Harry's proposal, she writes the following letter and mails it immediately:

Deer Hairy,

I cud naver mary a lily-liverd, yeller-belleed cowerd like you. Gud ridence.

Daisy Mae

Unfortunately, on the very next day, Arnold is severely injured in one of those all too common thresher accidents. Realizing that Arnold will no longer be able to pull the plow, Daisy Mae calls Harry immediately to accept his offer of marriage. A few days later, Harry receives

Daisy Mae's letter.

In this case, Daisy Mae validly accepted Harry's offer before her rejection. Therefore, her rejection will be ignored (well, probably not by Harry).

Counter Offers

If the person receiving the offer makes a counter offer, then the law treats the counter offer as a rejection of the original offer and the making of a brand new offer. As a result, once you make a counter offer, you are no longer free to accept the original offer.

For instance, let's suppose Bachelor Bill asks Stacked Susan to go out for dinner, dancing and a nightcap. Susan responds that she would like to go to dinner but no dancing and *definitely* no nightcap. In this case, she has rejected his original offer and made a counter offer. As a result, Bill is no longer obligated to take her out at all.

A more subtle question that confronts many guys is whether they are still obligated to take the woman out if she responds that she would like to go out with them, but "just as friends."

CONSIDERATION

Consideration is the thing of value exchanged in the contract. In a purchase and sale contract, the buyer is exchanging her money for a product and the seller is exchanging that product for money. In most cases, there can be no valid contract without *adequate consideration.*

As a result, a court will not usually enforce a promise of a gift (these are called "*donative promises*"). This is not to say that the law doesn't recognize gifts or that they are illegal. However, a judge won't force you to make good on a promised gift.

For instance, if you call the Jerry Lewis Telethon and pledge $1 million to Jerry's Kids, you don't have to pay the money. This is because Jerry's Kids didn't provide any consideration for your donation.

NOTE FROM THE PUBLISHER: Lawpsided Press does NOT encourage you to make phony donations to charity. It is immature, immoral and just not funny! At least, that's what

---

Common Nightclub Counter Offers

Offer: "How about a little kiss?"
Counter: "How about a black eye?"

Offer: "Why don't we take a little walk together?"
Counter: "Why don't you take a hike?"

Offer: "Your place or mine?"
Counter: <SLAP!>

the Lewis Telethon said after our $386 million "donation" last year.

As always, there are exceptions to the consideration requirement. One exception is the concept of *promissory estoppel* or *detrimental reliance*. Under this concept, a court will enforce a donative promise if the promised-to-party (the *promisee*) relies on the promise to his detriment.

For example, let's suppose Larry the Loser has spent years floating aimlessly from job to job. Larry's parents become concerned about his future and promise to send him to college. Larry is excited at the news and runs to his boss at Burger World and tells him to shove those french fries ... (well, you know the rest). Two weeks later, Larry's parents change their minds and decide not to send him to college.

Normally, Larry's parents' promise would be unenforceable because it was not backed by consideration. However, since Larry relied on this promise to his detriment, he *theoretically* would be entitled to a college education. In reality, Larry's parents would probably just have to compensate him for his lost wages. Therefore, for some period of time, Larry's parents would have to pay him $30 per week and all the fries he could eat.

In many cases, courts will simply compensate the promisee for any loss suffered rather than strictly enforcing the promise. However, what happens when the promisee *positively relies* on the promise?

For instance, let's suppose Nicotine Nancy's parents are concerned about her smoking habit. They promise to buy her a new car if she quits smoking. Relying on this promise, Nancy kicks the habit. Ironically, her parents start smoking themselves and can no longer afford to buy her a new car because they now spend all their money on cigarettes.

If Nancy sues her parents for breaking their promise, she can't really claim that she *detrimentally* relied upon their promise to buy her a new car. Quitting smoking has probably made her healthier and saved her money. Therefore, a judge may rule that Nancy has received enough of a benefit and therefore, she shouldn't be entitled to a new car as well.

Chapter in Review
Formation of a Contract

1.   To be valid, an offer must:

    a.   Be void where prohibited

    b.   Be one you can't refuse

    c.   Describe the agreement in meaningful detail

2.   The Mailbox Rule states:

    a.   An acceptance is effective upon dispatch

    b.   An acceptance is effective upon receipt

    c.   30% of your mail will be addressed to the previous occupant

3.   Which of the following is adequate legal consideration for a contract?

    a.   Love

    b.   Money

    c.   Enron stock

Chapter 2

DEFENSES TO FORMATION
Finding a Loophole

By now, you know that the law is riddled with exceptions. Therefore, even if all elements of formation have been satisfied – offer, acceptance and consideration – there are a number of defenses to the formation of a valid contract.

Before explaining each of these defenses in detail, it is important to understand their effects. In some cases, a defense to formation will *void* the contract. As a result, all parties must return whatever was given to them in the contract. This is called *rescission* of the contract. In other cases, the defense will make the contract *voidable* by one of the parties. If the contract is voidable, then one party *may* cancel the contract but is not required to do so. This allows her to have the benefit of the contract if things turn out well and rescission of the contract if things don't turn out so well.

CAPACITY

A basic requirement of contract law is that both parties must have the *capacity* to understand the contract. If one party is unable to understand the contract because of insanity, mental defect or being educated in our public school system, then the contract is voidable by that party.

Likewise, if one of the parties is a minor, then the contract is voidable by the minor. However, minors can't go around voiding contracts with impunity. For instance, if a minor buys a stereo on credit and then decides to void the contract, he will have to return the stereo.

Also, contracts for necessities, such as food and shelter, are <u>not</u> voidable. Therefore, a landlord may enter a valid apartment lease with a mentally ill person, which is how I got my first apartment.

Lastly, if one of the parties is unable to understand the contract because of a temporary condition, then that person may void the contract if it is for non-necessities. For example, let's suppose Marijuana Mike sells you his car in exchange for a giant bag of potato chips. When Mike finally gets over the munchies, he may rescind the contract and get his car back. On the other hand, he may decide that he was better off with the bag of potato chips than with his 1976 Chevy Chevette.

PUBLIC POLICY

All states have established that certain contracts are unenforceable in their courts.

Illegality

A common example is contracts for illegal purposes, such as gambling. Therefore, the courts will not step in to make sure that your bookie pays off. In fact, the courts will not even step in to void the contract and return your original wager.

Unconscionability

Also, a court will not enforce contract terms that are *unconscionable*, or really unfair. Of course, defining a term like "unconscionable" is much like defining the terms "beauty," "love" or "sexual relations with that woman." It is a matter of opinion.

Historically, courts were reluctant to judge the fairness of a deal, particularly in terms of price. However, in recent years, courts have been more willing to void contracts on the grounds of unconscionability.

For example, let's suppose a young boy named Jack is sent into town by his mother to sell their cow. Being young and naïve, Jack sells the cow for a handful of magic beans. In this case, Jack's mother may sue to recover the cow because everyone knows that a cow is worth at least *two* handfuls of magic beans.

Contract Terms That Should Be Unconscionable

- Charging a $15 fee for a bounced check (if I had an extra $15, I wouldn't have bounced the check in the first place)

- Requiring 4 years of payments for a new car when the new car smell is gone after 2 months

- Requiring repayment of school loans when there are no practical uses for a Ph.D. in Medieval History

- Charging $50 to get into an amusement park and forcing customers to wait in lines longer than the Great Wall of China, only slower moving

---

FRAUD

Fraud occurs when one party is *tricked* into the contract by lies. Take the following purely hypothetical example. Let's suppose that a certain witty, intelligent and sexy author convinces people to buy a certain book by promising that it explains legal principles in a humorous way. If the book does not live up to this promise, then the purchasers of the book are just stuck with it because trust me, I have already spent your money.

NOTE FROM THE PUBLISHER: We have already spent your money too!

Seriously, you may void a contract if the other party lies to you and you rely on those lies to enter into the contract. The same is true even if the other party doesn't lie but rather just omits important facts.

For instance, let's suppose a salesman at Transistor Town sells you a TV set *without* informing you of known defects, such as it was manufactured in America. If the TV stops working (and it will), you may void the contract. Unless, of course, you also knew that the TV was made in America.

DURESS

A contract is also voidable if one party is *coerced* into the contract by force or threat of physical harm. For instance, let's suppose Sammy the Switchblade makes you "an offer you can't refuse." In this case, you may void the contract (although I wouldn't recommend doing so).

In addition, there is a concept of *economic duress*. This is where one party is coerced into agreement by threat of serious financial injury. For instance, let's suppose you hire a personal injury lawyer to sue McDonald's for allowing you to burn yourself with hot coffee. However, your lawyer waits until the day before your claim runs out before filing your lawsuit. He then tells you that he will file the case but only for *triple* his normal fee. At this point, you agree because otherwise, you will have no right to collect $25 *trillion* from McDonald's. In this case, after bankrupting McDonald's, you can void the lawyer's fee increase.

MISTAKE

In some cases, one party is mistaken about some important fact concerning the contract. In this case, the contract is voidable by that party. I guess ignorance really is bliss.

For instance, let's suppose Jokester Jim sells a plaid suit to Blind Barney telling him that it's an "Italian original." As you

can see, this suit constitutes the greatest crime against fashion since Cher's last appearance at an awards show. When Barney's friends finally gain the courage to tell him the truth, he will be able to return the suit to Jim.

Sometimes, the parties will enter into a contract on the basis of a mutual mistake. In this case, the contract will be enforced only if the parties assumed the risk of mistake.

For instance, let's suppose that an old mountain man named Jed (who barely kept his family fed) purchases a plot of land in exchange for a batch of Granny's "home brew." The very next day, while out hunting for some food, he comes across a spot of bubbling crude ... oil that is ... black gold ... Texas tea. Although Jed and the former owner of the land were mistaken as to its true value, the former owner may not void the contract. This is because buyers and sellers of real estate assume the risk that the property may be worth more or less than the contract price.

On the other hand, let's suppose you arrange to buy a goose on eBay for $50. While the seller is loading the goose into his truck, it lays a *golden* egg. Obviously, at this point, the seller doesn't want to sell the goose to you anymore (at least not for $50).

In this case, neither of you assumed any risk that the goose would be worth

much more or less than $50. As a result, the seller will probably be able to void the contract. Interestingly, had the purchase been completed before discovering that the goose was "The Goose That Lays the Golden Eggs," you could have kept the goose.

THE STATUTE OF FRAUDS

Most contracts need not be in writing. However, each state requires certain contracts to be in writing. Ironically, the state laws listing these contracts are called "The Statutes of Frauds."

The basic categories of contracts that must be in writing are:

- contracts made in consideration for marriage (not the actual marriage contract)

- contracts that can't be fully performed within one year

- contracts involving real estate (including leases)

- promises by executors to pay estate debts out of their personal funds

- contracts for the sale of goods priced at $500 or more

- guarantees of another person's obligations (sureties)

In law school, our Contracts professor taught us to remember this list by using the acronym, MY LEGS – **M**arriage, **Y**ear, **L**and, **Ex**ecutors, **G**oods, **S**urety. In theory, this was a sound learning device. Unfortunately, our professor had *great* legs. As a result, whenever the male students thought of *her* LEGS, the Statute of Frauds was the last thing on our minds.

Parol Evidence

An interesting legal rule in this context is the *parol evidence rule*. The basic principle is that *parol* (oral) evidence can't be introduced to contradict a written agreement.

For instance, let's suppose you enter into a written sales agreement that states, "All Sales are Final." In this case, theoretically you are barred from claiming that the salesperson promised a *50-year* money-back guarantee. However, there are a number of exceptions to this rule. In fact, the rule is riddled with so many exceptions that it has about as much legal significance as the rule that requires you to wait 30 minutes after eating to resume swimming.

Chapter in Review
Defenses to Formation

1. A person is "incapable" of entering into a valid contract if:

    a. He is a minor

    b. He has credit as bad as mine

    c. His mother still picks out his clothes for him

2. The term "unconscionable" refers to:

    a. Ted Kennedy at 12:01 a.m. on New Years' Day

    b. Members of the audience after an Al Gore speech

    c. Contract terms that are extremely unfair

3. Which law requires certain contracts to be in writing?

    a. The Statute of Limitations

    b. The Statute of Frauds

    c. The Statue of Liberty

Chapter 3

PERFORMANCE
"But Ma, Do I Have To?"

Let's assume you've formed a valid contract to which there are no defenses. The question now is whether you *have* to perform your obligations under the contract? Interestingly, the answer is "maybe not." There are still ways to weasel out of the contract.

CONDITIONS

In some cases, you only become obligated to act *af-ter* some other event occurs. For instance, over the years, many women have agreed to go out with me *when* Hell freezes over. As a result, none of these women is obligated to go out with me *yet*. However, when Hell finally freezes over -- *watch out!*

In some cases, the contract doesn't specify who must perform first. To prevent these transactions

from turning into shouting matches of "You go first!" "No, *you* go first!", the law requires both sides to perform simultaneously whenever possible. For example, in the typical purchase and sale transaction, payment will be due upon the delivery of the product.

However, when one party is providing labor in return for money, the labor is performed first and the money is paid upon completion of the work. This is why most employees get paid only for the period of time that they've *already* worked. The same is true for contractors, such as builders and mechanics.

To protect workers, many state laws impose hefty fines against employers who don't pay their workers on time. Also, builders and contractors are often granted statutory liens against the property worked on if the owner doesn't pay for their services.

Nevertheless, some laborers will require money in advance for their services. After all, a masseuse is going to have trouble obtaining a mechanic's lien on your *back*.

DISCHARGE

If performing your end of the bargain would be illegal, impossible, impracticable, or fattening, your obligation will be discharged. Of course, in this case, you will be required to return any consideration received from the other party.

Illegality

For instance, let's suppose Daisy Mae and the kinfolk convince the popular gangsta rapper, Ice Cream, to perform at a local concert in exchange for $50 and all of the corn liquor he can drink. However, before the concert can take place, the county passes a law prohibiting rap music. As a result, Daisy Mae and the kinfolk are no longer required to sell *all* their earthly possessions to pay Ice Cream the agreed upon fee. Likewise, Ice Cream is now free to perform his triple platinum hit, "Ghetto Booty," elsewhere.

Impossibility

Also, a contract will be discharged if one of the parties dies or the property to be worked upon is destroyed. For instance, let's suppose I agree to paint your house on Sunday.

Unfortunately, your house burns down on Saturday night. As a result, I am no longer obligated to paint your house and can now spend my Sunday at the Ice Cream concert. On the other hand, you are also excused from paying me. Therefore, even if I really need the money (and trust me, I do), I can't show up at your house and start painting the ground where your house used to be and demand payment.

Impracticability

A contract also may be discharged on the grounds that performance is *impracticable*. Please note that impracticability is more than mere inconvenience. For instance, my obligation to paint your house will not be discharged on the grounds of impracticability just because I have a hangover. Nor will my obligation be discharged if I lose my truck in a poker game on Saturday night. Legally, in this case, I would be required to load all my painting equipment on the bus, if necessary. On the other

hand, I would be excused if the area was suddenly hit by a tornado.

Also, impracticability does not excuse performance just because of a change in market conditions. For instance, let's suppose I agree to buy my son a Teenage Cabbage Elmo Furby for Christmas if he stops hitting his little brother over the head with the telephone. Let's further suppose that Teenage Cabbage Elmo Furby becomes the hottest selling toy of the Christmas season and now costs double its original price. In this case, I am still obligated to wait in 14-hour lines to buy it for him.

On the other hand, if the price of the toy rises *astronomically* and it can be purchased only on eBay at a price equal to the national debt, I will be excused from making good on my promise. However, I will have to let my son go back to hitting his little brother with the telephone again. As you can see, parenthood is full of strange compromises.

ANTICIPATORY BREACH

Finally, a person may be excused from performance because of an *anticipatory breach* by the other party. In other words, you are not obligated to perform if the other party is unable or unwilling to perform.

Otherwise, you would have to perform your end of the bargain and then immediately sue the other party for breach. Obviously, this is contrary to common sense. This is unless, of course, you are accustomed to dealing with contractors, insurance companies and used car dealers.

For instance, let's suppose you agree to buy a car from your neighbor's sister's boyfriend. If he shows up to close the deal without the pink slip or the car, you don't hand over your money.

Likewise, let's suppose the roles are reversed and you are selling the car instead of buying it. If the buyer attempts to pay you with a third-party check written on a bank in Somalia, you don't have to hand over the keys.

Just remember though, the law requires you to be *reasonable* in determining that the other party will breach the agreement. Also, the breach must be significant.

For instance, you can't breach just because the other party was three *minutes* late to the closing. Nor can you refuse to buy the car just because it has a *tiny* ding on the hood. However, you may refuse to buy the car if it is on fire.

Chapter in Review
Performance

1. A party may be discharged from a contract if:
    a. He violates the "don't ask, don't tell" policy
    b. He has a really good lawyer
    c. Performing the contract is illegal, impossible or impracticable

2. In a personal services contract, who must perform first?
    a. The party providing the service
    b. The party receiving the service
    c. The party who needs the contract most

3. Which of the following is a valid reason for anticipatory breach?
    a. You get a better deal elsewhere
    b. The other party files bankruptcy
    c. You get a "really bad feeling about this one"

Chapter 4

REMEDIES
Doing Things the Hard Way

If one party doesn't keep his end of the bargain, then the other party will be entitled to damages in court. This chapter discusses the various forms of damages available for breach of contract.

LIQUIDATED DAMAGES

In some cases, the contract will state that if one party breaches the contract, then the other party is entitled to a specific amount of damages. These are called "liquidated damages." One example of liquidated damages is the late fee charged by video stores. If you don't return the video by the due date, you will be assessed a late fee.

Late fees are perfectly legal unless they are unreasonable. Therefore, Brickbuster Video can't charge $3,000 in late fees just because you were a few days late returning *Shrek*.

EXPECTATION DAMAGES

In the absence of liqui-dated damages, a court will usually award *expectation damages*. Expectation damages are calculated to make the other party whole. Or, in other words, to put her in the same position she would have been in had you kept your end of the deal.

In contracts for the sale of goods, the seller is entitled to his expected profit from the sale. For example, let's suppose Wiley William enters into an agreement to sell 1,000 candy bars to the local convenience store at 50¢ per bar ($500 total). He then purchases the candy bars at Costco for 25¢ per bar ($250).

In the meantime, the convenience store owner discovers Costco himself and refuses to purchase the candy bars from William. If William brings a lawsuit, he will be entitled to expectation damages of his expected profit of $250.

If the seller breaches the contract, then he must reimburse the buyer for any added expenses in obtaining the goods from a third party. For instance, let's suppose Wholesale Wally decides to surprise his girlfriend with a watch for Valentine's Day. However, rather than buying the watch at a retail establishment, Wally arranges to buy the watch at the "wholesale" price of $50 from Shady Sam.

Unfortunately, Sam is arrested shortly before Valentine's Day in the largest stolen property fencing operation not actually involving my brother-in-law. As a result, Sam can't deliver the watch and Wally is forced to pay the retail price of $500. If Wally sues Sam for breach of contract, then he may be able to recover $450 -- the difference between the retail price and wholesale price.

Nevertheless, in this case, Wally is not likely to sue Sam. After all, Wally may be subject to criminal prosecution for attempting to purchase stolen property. And he definitely will be subject to *girlfriend persecution* for attempting to buy his Valentine's Day gift at wholesale.

In service contracts, the laborer is entitled to lost wages and the cost of materials. For instance, let's suppose Crackhead Cameron hires you to repair his TV set for $100. When you arrive at Cameron's home, you learn that he has just sold his TV set for $10. Since there is no TV to repair, you decide to take the rest of the day off and smoke crack with Cameron (if you can't beat 'em, join 'em). If you later sue Cameron for breach of contract, you will be entitled to $100 in expectation damages *minus* the value of the crack you smoked.

However, please note that as a laborer, you do have a duty to seek other employment, if possible. Therefore, if you could have fixed another TV set during the time you were smoking crack with Cameron, then you can't collect expectation damages from him. But let's get real; you aren't going to *collect* damages from Cameron anyway.

NOTE FROM THE PUBLISHER: Despite the last two paragraphs, we would like to point out that drugs are no laughing matter. Moreover, Lawpsided Press does not *in any way* support or condone the use of drugs *of any kind*. This message is brought to you in part by our sponsors -- Philip Morris, Anheiser Busch and Starbucks.

CONSEQUENTIAL DAMAGES

In some cases, one party will suffer other damages as a result of the breach. These are called "consequential damages." For instance, if Always Late Airlines strands you overnight in New Jersey, you will have to pay for a hotel room. If the delay was caused by the airline, then it must reimburse you for the cost of the room.

As a general rule, the breaching party is only liable for consequential damages if it could have easily foreseen them. For instance, it is easily foreseeable that a stranded traveler will need to pay for a hotel room. Therefore, these damages are recoverable as consequential damages.

However, let's suppose you were flying to New York for an interview at a big law firm but the delay caused

you to miss the interview and not get the job. In this case, you can't sue the airline for the millions of dollars you *may* have earned over the next 40 years at the firm. This is because your losses in this case were not so easily foreseeable by the airline. However, the airline will have to reimburse you for damages if you are robbed at gunpoint while stranded in New Jersey because that was *easily* foreseeable.

WELCOME TO NEW JERSEY

RELIANCE DAMAGES

As discussed earlier, in some cases, a party may recover damages if he relies on the promise of the other party to his detriment. For instance, let's suppose Flaky Felicia agrees to go out on a date with Sloppy Sam. In anticipation of the date, Sam buys items he wouldn't normally purchase, such as a toothbrush, comb, soap and new underwear. If Felicia later cancels the date, then Sam is theoretically entitled to the money he spent in preparation for the date.

NOTE FROM THE AUTHOR: Guys, please do not sue a woman because she stands you up. Our court system is already bogged down with enough silly lawsuits. Moreover, doing so will really make you look like a dork.

RESTITUTION

Even if there is no valid contract, courts will sometimes award *restitution* to compensate for unjust enrichment. For example, let's suppose Dyslexic Danny has made an agreement to paint a house located at 1212 Lemon Drive. Unfortunately, Danny goes to a house located at *2121 Melon* Drive instead. The owner of this house, Cheap Charlie, just sits by and watches Danny paint his house.

As a general rule, Danny wouldn't be entitled to payment because there was no contract between him and Charlie. However, in this case, because Charlie has been *unjustly enriched*, Danny can recover the value of his services.

However, please don't think you can boost your "sales" by providing work for unwilling customers and then suing them for restitution. Danny would only be successful in his case because Charlie was aware of Danny's mistake and made no effort to stop him. Had Charlie not been at home at the time, Danny would not have been entitled to payment.

SPECIFIC PERFORMANCE

As a general rule, the courts will only grant monetary damages. However, in limited cases, the courts will require you to *specifically perform* your obligations under the contract. Strangely enough, the term for this type of remedy is "specific performance."

Specific performance is usually only available where monetary damages are inadequate. For instance, in real estate contracts, a breaching seller may be compelled to transfer the property because each parcel of land is unique. The same thing would be true for other rare items, such as family heirlooms, antiques and purchased copies of this book.

However, in personal services contracts, specific performance is almost never awarded. Therefore, even if your barber walks out in the middle of your haircut, he won't be forced to finish it. The only time when specific performance will be enforced is when the person is being compelled not to take some action, such as compete with a former employer.

For instance, let's suppose you take a job working for a company. As part of the mountain of paperwork you sign on your first day, you execute a Non-Compete Agreement. In this agreement, you promise that if you leave the company, you will not compete for the company's customers for some period (e.g., until the end of time). Let's further suppose you leave the company to start your own company in the same field.

In some states, the Non-Compete Agreement would be enforceable. As a result, you would be prevented from competing with your former company for some period of time.

REFORMATION

In some cases, courts will modify a contract to make it accurately reflect the true intentions of the parties. For instance, let's suppose two friends, Skeeter and Cooter, go into the recycling business. Not wanting to cut into their profits by employing "city slicker" lawyers, they draft up their own partnership agreement, which reads as follows:

I, Skeeter, and him, Cooter, agree to recical all our bear cans and split the munny 40-40.

At the end of the first week, they collectively drink and recycle *450* cans of beer, which results in recycling returns of $22.50.

Unfortunately, since neither man advanced past the 4th grade, they have trouble equally dividing the money. Rather than shoot each other, which is the town custom, they take their dispute to the local justice of the peace. The justice may reform the contract so that it reads that Skeeter and Cooter will split the *money 50-50* from recycling *beer* cans.

Chapter in Review
Remedies

1. **What are liquidated damages?**
    a.   Unpaid bar tabs
    b.   Furniture damage after a wild party
    c.   Specific damages provided for in the contract

2. **What is the purpose of expectation damages?**
    a.   To make the non-breaching party whole
    b.   To make the breaching party whole
    c.   To make each party go "halvsies"

3. **Which of the following is an example of restitution?**
    a.   A prostitute's vacation at Club Med
    b.   A home for retired workaholics
    c.   None of the above

Chapter 5

EFFECTS ON THIRD PARTIES
Dealing With the Party of the Third Part

THIRD-PARTY BENEFICIARIES

In some contracts, one party will promise to perform for the benefit of a third party. For example, let's suppose your husband agrees to make you breakfast in bed every day for a week. In exchange, you agree to be nice to his mother during her next visit, no matter how many times she insinuates that you have no clue of how to take care of her "baby." If your husband lives up to his part of the bargain, then you are obligated to be nice to his mother.

If you fail to do so, then he could sue you for damages. In addition, his mother could drag you into court for breach of contract. And wouldn't she just love to do that! Believe it or not, as a third-party beneficiary to your contract with her "baby," she has rights under the contract.

However, it should be noted that a person is only a third-party beneficiary if the parties intend her to be one. In this case, it was clear that you were to live up to your end of the bargain by being nice to your mother-in-law. Your obligation is specific to her. Therefore, your poor father-in-law can't sue you, even though he will have to suffer through your mother-in-law's complaints about you *every day* for the rest of his life.

Now, you know why men die so much earlier than women ... they want to!

ASSIGNMENT

In some cases, one party will wish to transfer his interest in the contract to a third party. A common example is when your bank sells your mortgage to another bank every three days. As a result, you become obligated to make all future payments to the new bank.

As a general matter, contracts are freely assignable unless they state otherwise. However, many contracts state that they may not be assigned or may be only assigned with the other party's consent.

Of course, some contracts, by their very nature, are not assignable. For instance, most personal services contracts are not assignable. As a result, Pamela Anderson can't assign her contract to appear in *Playboy* to Linda Tripp. This limitation on assignment proves two things: (1) the law sometimes makes good sense and (2) THERE IS A GOD!

Finally, please note that even if you assign your interest in a contract, you retain some obligations under the contract. Therefore, if the assignee does not perform, you are still responsible for performing. For example, let's suppose Brave Bobby *agrees* to take on the task of clipping his grandfather's toenails ("family values" are sometimes overrated). After two months of near-death experiences and horrific nightmares, Bobby pays his 5-year-old sister, Fearless Francine, to do the job for him.

However, Bobby's nightmares may not be over yet. If Francine is injured from sharp, flying nails during her "tour of duty," Bobby will be required to re-enlist.

Chapter in Review
Effects on Third Parties

1. What is a third-party beneficiary?

   a. What you hope to be in your rich uncle's will

   b. Pat Buchanon's running mate

   c. Someone who is not party to a contract but has rights under the contract anyway

TORTS
(Personal Injury Law)
WHEN SAYING YOU'RE SORRY JUST ISN'T ENOUGH

TORTS
OVERVIEW

Before beginning a discussion of the law of torts, it is important to answer the question of "what is a tort?" In short, a tort is any bad act that isn't a breach of contract.

For example, let's suppose your best friend, Jumbo Jim, accidentally steps on your foot. Unfortunately for you, Jim weighs *500* pounds. You decide that the best way to get even with him is to take him to court. However, since accidentally stepping on your foot isn't a *crime*, you can't have him arrested. Besides, the police couldn't fit him into a squad car anyway. Moreover, as you don't have a contract with Jim where he promised to never step on your foot, you can't sue him for *breach of contract*. Therefore, in order to sue him, you must bring an action under tort law.

Of course, to bring a lawsuit based on a tort, you must have a legal theory to support your claim. Fortunately, in America, the theory need not be logical or even remotely reasonable but you must have a theory just the same.

The following chapters explain the standard theories of tort law. And if you pay careful attention, you may end up like this *very* satisfied reader.

Before reading this book, I was working two jobs and living from paycheck to paycheck. However, through the tips learned in this chapter, I was able to go from slip-and-fall to slip-and-own. I am now the proud owner of 237 retail-shopping outlets nationwide! And it wouldn't have been possible without this book! I can't thank you enough!

Macy Saks

Chapter 6

INTENTIONAL TORTS
Sometimes Accidents Happen On Purpose

An intentional tort is any harm committed either *purposefully* or with the knowledge that injury is *substantially certain to occur.* For instance, let's suppose Bitter Bob purposefully drives his car onto a crowded sidewalk. If someone is injured, then Bob has committed an intentional tort because of the substantial certainty that someone would be injured by his actions. Of course, this is not true in Massachusetts, where driving on the sidewalk seems to be allowed, and even encouraged.

Also, you can commit an intentional tort even if the harm caused is not the harm intended. For example, let's suppose you *intend* to hit your friend with a water balloon at the company picnic. However, you miss and hit the boss' wife, ruining her new outfit. In addition to being fired, you may be sued for intentional tort because your intent to hit your friend will be transferred to the boss' wife.

CRIMINAL CONDUCT

Assaults, batteries and most other crimes are intentional torts. In addition to being subject to criminal punishment, the offender is liable for tort damages.

An interesting example of a criminal tort is false imprisonment. The crime of false imprisonment occurs when the victim is confined by a physical barrier or by force or threats.

Surprisingly, false imprisonment tort cases arise fairly frequently. The most likely scenario is where the victim is accidentally locked inside the defendant's place of business overnight. In this type of case, the primary question is whether the defendant knew or should have known that someone was locked inside his business.

For instance, let's suppose three castaways from the TV show *Survivor* meet for lunch just after taping the final episode. After surviving the previous seven weeks on bugs, rats and memories of food, they head for the nearest all-you-can-eat buffet. *Twelve hours later*, two of the castaways leave the restaurant, smiling and using table legs as toothpicks. The restaurant owner notices that one castaway is no longer with them, but just assumes that she was eaten along with the rest of the patrons. The owner then locks up the restaurant for the night *without* checking for survivors.

The next morning, the owner arrives at the restaurant to find the missing castaway drinking directly from the ice cream machine. As a technical

matter, this castaway could sue the owner for false imprisonment because he failed to check the dining area, the restrooms, the refrigerator or inside the salad bar for any remaining patrons.

EMOTIONAL DISTRESS

Another claim in tort law is the intentional infliction of emotional distress. This claim is very often stacked upon other intentional tort claims. For instance, a *plaintiff* (the person who brings the lawsuit) suing for assault will often make a separate claim for intentional infliction of emotional distress against the *defendant* (the person being sued).

However, in some cases, emotional distress is a completely separate ground for the lawsuit. This is the case when the defendant's conduct is so outrageous that no *reasonable person* could bear it, such as singing Britney Spears songs while stuck in a crowded elevator (or at any time, for that matter).

However, the conduct must be *really* outrageous. Mere insults, profanity or bad manners are not enough to constitute intentional infliction of emotional stress. For instance, Michael Stivic from *All in the Family* couldn't sue Archie Bunker for constantly calling him "Meathead". This is particularly true considering that, over the years, Rob Reiner's head has become rather meaty.

DEFAMATION

The torts of libel and slander both involve mak-

ing *defamatory* statements about someone. The only difference between them is that libel occurs when the statements are written and slander occurs when the statements are spoken.

A statement is defamatory if it negatively affects someone's reputation. However, once again, mere name-calling is not enough to injure someone's reputation. Therefore, simply saying that "Lisa is a witch!" is not defamatory. However, backing up this statement with specific reasons as to why Lisa is a witch may be defamatory.

Moreover, there are some statements that are so obviously harmful to a person's reputation that the law classifies them as automatically, or *per se*, defamatory. The categories of *per se* defamation are:

- **Negative statements about someone's business practices** (e.g., "Joe is a crook!")

- **Statements that someone has a loathsome disease** (e.g., "Bobby has the cooties!")

- **Statements that someone has commit-**
ted a terrible crime (e.g., "O.J. killed my sister!")

- **Statements that a woman sleeps around** (e.g., "Julie is a slut!")

Of course, it is not defamatory to claim that a *man* sleeps around. Nor is it even necessary to make such a claim. After all, if a man sleeps around, he will take it upon himself to make sure that *everyone* knows about it.

Also, a defamatory statement doesn't have to be a direct attack. Innuendo can be defamatory. For instance, let's suppose Racist Randy whispers to his neighbor, "Did you hear what happened to Joe's dog? Well, just put it this way, I'd keep my dogs out of the Nguyen's yard if I were you ... unless you want Rover to end up in the moo goo gai pan." In this case, even though Randy didn't directly accuse the Nguyens of eating Joe's dog, he certainly implied it and therefore, he has defamed them.

Also, for a statement to be defamatory, it must be directed at a particular person or very small group of people. Therefore, stating that the French are rude, cocky and smelly is <u>not</u> defamatory, just true.

Finally, defamatory statements can't be made about a dead person. Well, to put it more accurately, you can't be sued for defaming a dead person. Therefore, we are all free to say anything we want about George Washington, Abraham Lincoln or Scott Baio.

NOTE FROM THE PUBLISHER: During our fact checking process, we discovered that Scott Baio is actually still alive. It's just his career that is dead.

DEFENSES

There are several defenses available to someone being sued for an intentional tort. One of the most obvious defenses is consent of the victim. Sometimes, consent is given explicitly. In other cases, consent can be implied.

For instance, a professional football player has implicitly consented to the physical contact involved in the game of football. Therefore, he may not sue an-

other player for tackling him, as tackling is part of the game.

However, he may sue another player for contact that is outside the scope of the game. For instance, a player may be sued for hugging another player or patting his butt. Unless, of

course, he does so to celebrate a touchdown, field goal or negative drug test.

Also, if the intentional tort is a crime, then any other defenses to the crime (e.g., self-defense, insanity, the "race card") are available to the defendant. In other words, if you have a valid defense in a criminal trial, then you may use that defense in a tort action.

A *Lawp*sided View
Libel

In 2001, a VW dealership sued a Georgia Tech graduate student, George Mantis, for statements made by Mantis on an Internet bulletin board.

Mr. Mantis described his unpleasant experiences with the dealership on VWvortex.com, a web site for VW enthusiasts. Apparently, the dealership became worried about the negative messages being received by the dozen or so daily visitors to this site. Therefore, in a stroke of genius only rivaled by Dan Quayle's spelling prowess, the dealership attracted more attention to the matter by taking Mantis to court.

For fear of being subject to my own libel suit, I will not name the dealership in question. However, I will give you a hint. Its name sounds a lot like with Jim Ellis MOFORS.

In this case, the dealership claimed that Mantis' postings damaged its reputation. And this claim would have some merit if it were not for one small problem – Jim Ellis MOFORS is a car dealership. Correct me if I'm wrong, but car salesmen are not exactly known for their honesty, integrity or even their ability to avoid jail time. After all, when was the last time you heard someone say, "That John is a saint – kind and honest – he should either become a priest or a used car salesman"?

Nevertheless, the dealership had a strong case for libel. The law deems some classes of statements as defamatory *per se* (which is Latin for Percy). Claiming that someone's business practices are unethical is one such class of statements.

In his defense, Mantis could argue that he didn't impugn the integrity of the dealership but rather simply retold the facts as they happened. Moreover, there are constitutional considerations at play here.

The statements at issue here were published on a web site and therefore, in the press. The First Amendment provides special protections for freedom of the press. As a result, the press is allowed extra leeway in reporting on public figures.

If Mantis had defamed a private person, he and the web site would be liable unless they could prove that the statements were true. However, since the dealership probably runs more spots on local television than that annoying little guy who promises that "you too can get rich by placing tiny classified ads in the newspaper," Jim Ellis MOFORS is likely a public figure.

As a result, unless Mantis knowingly posted a false message on the bulletin board, he will not be held liable for libel. In any event, this case should remind each of us to be more careful about what we say on internet bulletin boards, chat rooms and on the phone when our spouses are listening in on the other line.

NOTE TO MY WIFE: For the last time, I did not say that your mother is an "old, fat cow." I said, "She is all that ... wow!"

Chapter in Review
Intentional Torts

1. Which of the following crimes is also an intentional tort?

    a.   Battery

    b.   Negligent homicide

    c.   Owning a minivan

2. Defamation is the act of:

    a.   Making a "poopy"

    b.   Making a statement that injures another person's reputation

    c.   Calling someone bad names

3. Slander is to libel as:

    a.   Laurel is to Hardy

    b.   Falsehood is to Truth

    c.   Spoken is to Written

Chapter 7

NEGLIGENCE
"It's Always Fun Until Someone Loses an Eye"

The concept in the last chapter, intentional torts, was fairly straightforward. I wish I could promise the same thing about the subject of this chapter – the theory of negligence.

Negligence is complicated but worth the effort to understand because this is where the money is. After all, you can't always depend upon someone to commit an intentional tort against you. And even if you are "intentionally torted," it is usually by some person who has less money than you do.

However, with negligence, the sky is the limit. The theory of negligence is that the defendant *breached* some *duty of care* and *negligently caused* you harm. Therefore, by being creative in finding a cause for your harm and by assigning a duty to the defendant that didn't exist before, you can make out like a bandit (or even like the Gores at the 2000 Democratic National Convention).

DUTIES OF CARE

As a general matter, every person owes a duty of care to everyone she may foreseeably come into contact with. The basic duty of care is to act *reasonably*.

However, in some cases, the defendant will owe a

special duty of care. For instance, professionals and specialists are held to a higher standard of care than mere reasonableness.

In other cases, the duty of care depends upon the relationship between the parties. For instance, if I'm driving with a passenger in my car, I must not only drive reasonably but also, warn him of known problems with my car.

Fortunately, this duty to warn only applies to *invited guests*. Therefore, if I am carjacked while driving through Los Angeles (which is likely), I need not warn the carjacker that my car stalls frequently and has no brakes. Of course, he is likely to make these discoveries himself as he *pushes* my car away from the scene of the crime.

Likewise, for landowners, the duty of care varies depending upon the relationship between the parties. For trespassers, the landowner only has a limited duty to warn of extremely hazardous conditions, such as dinosaurs roaming the property or his mother-in-law sunbathing in a thong bikini.

However, if the property is open to the general public, then the landowner must make the extra effort to also discover hidden dangers. Therefore, Disneyland must ensure all rides are in proper working order and Mickey Mouse has had all of his shots.

Lastly, as a general matter, a person doesn't have a duty to rescue others. However, if a person attempts to make a rescue, he must do so reasonably. For instance, let's suppose Dirty Harry sees a dog locked in a parked car with the windows rolled up. As a matter of tort law, Dirty Harry doesn't have a duty

The Reasonable Person Standard

Although the reasonable person standard is supposed to be an "objective" standard, it is often judged by what is reasonable for a person just like the defendant. Therefore, the "reasonable person" standard, when applied to my actions, would be more like the "reasonable, brilliant, sexy, witty, 34-year old black man" standard. However, there is no such thing as a reasonable woman standard because of the lack of comparable examples.

to rescue the dog. However, Dirty Harry is not that kind of guy. Therefore, he frees the dog by blowing out the car windows with his .44 Magnum.

Unfortunately, Dirty Harry gets a little carried away (as usual) and blows up the entire car and several surrounding buildings. In this scenario, Dirty Harry would be negligent and could be sued by the vehicle's owner, the owners of the buildings, and anyone who has ever suffered through one of his movies.

BREACHING THE DUTY OF CARE

To prove negligence, the plaintiff must prove that the defendant did not live up to the duty of care owed by that defendant. This can be demonstrated in several ways.

Failure to Follow Standard Practice

In some cases, the plaintiff meets this burden of proof by demonstrating that the defendant didn't follow standard practice in his profession. For instance, let's suppose Eccentric Eddie works as a bus driver. Although most bus drivers actually *stop* the bus to allow passengers to get off, Eddie insists that his passengers leap from the bus as he slows it to a roll.

If someone is injured while leaping from his bus, Eddie would be found negligent everywhere in America except New York City, where the standard practice is to force passengers to leap from the bus while it travels at speeds in excess of the speed of light.

Violations of the Law

In other cases, the defendant breaches the duty of care if he acts illegally. For instance, let's suppose your landlord, Sammy Slumlord, fails to maintain proper lighting in the hallway of your apartment building, as required by law. If you fall down the stairs while groping through the dark hallway one night, Sammy will be found negligent.

Res Ipsa Loquitor

In other cases, the plaintiff may prove a breach of the duty of care through the doctrine of *res ipsa loquitor*, which is Latin for "the thing speaks for itself." This doctrine is used when the accident could have only occurred if someone was negligent and that someone could not have been anyone but the defendant.

A great illustration of this doctrine in action occurs during Episode #37 of *The Brady Bunch*. During this episode, Peter breaks a vase while playing ball in the house despite the fact that "Mom always said, 'Don't play ball in the house.'"

Brady Bunch Law

The Brady Bunch taught many legal principles in addition to *res ipsa loquitor*. The show taught the concepts of assumption of the risk and *caveat emptor*, which is Latin for "I'm out of caviar!" Nevertheless, the show possessed one legal flaw. In the Brady household, six children shared one bathroom. This must have been a violation of some health code!

When Mrs. Brady discovers that her vase is broken, she immediately suspects the kids through the doctrine of *res ipsa loquitor*. After all, vases don't *usually* break themselves. As the kids were in the house at the time, they were held responsible for breaking it and grounded. Believe it or not, this same reasoning is often applied in our courtrooms.

CAUSATION

Obviously, to be liable in tort, the defendant must have *legally caused* the harm. However, explaining the concept of legal causation is almost as difficult as justifying why I charge $400 per hour for my legal services.

For instance, let's suppose you are blind-sided at an intersection by another driver on your way to work. It seems pretty clear the other driver *caused* the accident. Therefore, his insurance company should cover your losses. Of course, this assumes that the other driver has automobile insurance. On the other hand, if you are hit by an uninsured motorist (i.e., any resident of Los Angeles County), then you will need to invent another "cause" of the accident.

Fortunately, this isn't as difficult as it may seem. *Theoretically*, every factor that contributed to both cars arriving at the intersection simultaneously is a "cause" of the accident. Therefore, it could be argued that the manufacturer of your alarm clock *caused* the accident because the clock's snooze button goes off every 9 minutes, instead of every 10 minutes. Likewise, the manufacturer of your car may have *caused* the accident because your car did not start until the third try that morning. Or perhaps, Howard Stern *caused* the accident by distracting the other driver with the wild antics of his morning radio show. And this is just a small sample of the possible *causes* for the accident.

With so many potential causes, how do you go about picking the proper cause and therefore, the proper defendant? Well, historically, the law looked to the "but-for" cause of the harm. This is the cause "but-for" which there would not have been an injury. However, over time, the "but-for" causation standard has evolved into the "but-he's-rich" standard.

As a result, the law now looks to the person who was the *proximate cause* of the harm. A person is the proximate cause of the harm if he breached a duty of care and it was reasonably foreseeable that harm would result.

Therefore, using our car

crash example above, in order for Howard Stern to be held responsible for the accident, the plaintiff would have to show that Howard breached a duty of care to the listening public and the breach caused the accident.

Obviously, this would be difficult to do. Although Howard Stern's radio show features some of the most outrageous conduct to actually occur outside of the Clinton White House, it would be difficult to argue that he is acting unreasonably *as a matter of law*. Nevertheless, this shouldn't dissuade you from suing him after your next automobile accident, flat tire or fight with your spouse.

DEFENSES

Contributory Negligence

One defense available to the defendant in a negligence action is that the plaintiff was *contributorily negligent*. Or, in other words, the plaintiff was also at fault. Historically, at-fault plaintiffs could not recover for their injuries. However, in recent years, most states have gone to a *comparative negligence* standard.

Under this standard, the plaintiff and defendant share the costs depending upon their relative levels of fault. For instance, if the plaintiff was 25% at fault, she will still recover 75% of her damages. However, in most states, the plaintiff won't recover *anything* if she is more at fault than the defendant.

Assumption of the Risk

Another defense is *assumption of the risk* by the plaintiff. If the plaintiff engaged in knowingly dangerous behavior, then he can <u>not</u> recover for his injuries. For instance, if I were to dip my ears in steak sauce and get into a boxing ring with Mike Tyson, I assume the loss of an ear. As a result, I can't sue the boxing promoter if Mike decides to have a mid-round "snack."

Assumption of the risk is a common defense used by operators of dangerous facilities, such as bungee-jumping apparatus, ski lifts and drive-through wedding chapels. As a result, these operators will often require their customers to sign statements demonstrating that they assume the risk of their behavior. For instance, a bungee-jumping operator may require its customers to sign the disclaimer on the next page.

However, the defendant need not go to this extreme to prove that the plaintiff assumed the risk. In fact, in some cases, an assumption of the risk is *implied*. For instance, let's suppose Marcia Brady goes to a baseball game and is struck in the nose with a foul ball, causing her to scream "My dose! My dose!" In this case, her assumption of the risk is implied because baseball fans assume the risk of foul balls (and lethal boredom). As a result, she can't recover damages for her lost date with the most popular boy on campus, Biff Johnson.

NOTE FROM THE PUBLISHER: For you Brady Bunch fanatics who are saying, "Hey, there was no Biff Johnson on the show," GET A LIFE! And don't write us! We know the boy's name was Doug Simpson. This was a test of your geekiness. Unfortunately, you *passed*!

Chapter in Review
Negligence

1. An expert's duty of care is:
   a. Higher than a layperson's duty of care
   b. Lower than a layperson's duty of care
   c. Expensive

2. Under a comparative negligence standard, if the plaintiff is 30% negligent then she may only recover:
   a. After several therapy sessions
   b. 30% of her damages
   c. 70% of her damages

3. What is negligence?
   a. Something you purchase from Victoria's Secret
   b. Stupidity (i.e., negative intelligence)
   c. A breach of a duty of care that causes injury

STRICT LIABILITY
"What's Fault Got to Do With It!"

In some situations, the law imposes a duty to act more than just reasonably. In these cases, a person has an *absolute* duty to make a condition safe. If he fails to live up to this duty, then an injured person may sue under the theory of *strict liability*.

Strict liability is only available in certain abnormally dangerous situations, such as manufacturing explosives, raising saber-toothed tigers or dating more than one woman at a time. In these situations, a person may be liable for damages even if he used the utmost care in trying to prevent harm.

For instance, the Colonel Sanders-looking character from the movie, *Jurassic Park*, would have been held strictly liable for the deaths of all the people eaten by dinosaurs in the movie, except, of course, for the lawyer. In this case, his liability wouldn't be reduced just because he tried *really* hard to keep the dinosaurs in their pens.

Fortunately, most of us do not genetically re-engineer dinosaurs. However, many of us do have dogs.

THE ONE-BITE RULE

As a general rule, owning a dog does not subject you to strict liability because dogs are not usually dangerous. However, there is a rule called the "one-bite rule." In short, until a dog has bitten someone, its owner is not subject to strict liability. However, after the first bite, the owner is put on notice that the dog is dangerous. Thereafter, the owner is strictly liable for all future bites. In essence, the owner (or rather the dog) gets one free bite, so make it count!

DEFENSES

Assumption of the risk is a defense to strict liability. Likewise, contributory and comparative negligence will work as defenses.

For instance, let's suppose that Stupid Sam visits the zoo with his family. In order to get the "perfect picture," he climbs into the lion's den. In this case, Sam shouldn't be able to sue the zoo if he is attacked because he *assumed the risk of his behavior* and was *contributorily negligent* in causing the harm. However, this won't prevent Sam from winning a multi-*billion* dollar verdict if he brings suit in California.

Chapter in Review
Strict Liability

1. Strict liability is:

   a. Bill Clinton's greatest skill

   b. Having very demanding parents

   c. A legal standard imposing automatic responsibility for harm caused by abnormally dangerous behavior

PRODUCTS LIABILITY
Going After the Big Fish

This is the chapter you've all been waiting for. In this chapter, I'll give you the key to the vault. Here is where you'll learn how to sue the people who have the money.

The basic rule in products liability law is that anyone injured by a *defective* product can recover damages from a manufacturer, distributor or supplier of that product ... or just anyone with a lot of money.

WHO CAN SUE

Historically, only the purchaser of a defective product could sue under products liability. Over time, the family members of the purchaser and other users of the product were allowed to sue. At present, anyone who could have *foreseeably* been injured by the product can sue.

DEFECTS

Manufacturing Defects

Obviously, a product is defective if it's manufac-

tured incorrectly. Anyone who bought an American car during the 70s or 80s knows all about manufacturing defects. For instance, when the steering wheel on your brand new Plymouth came off in your hand as you drove away from the lot, that was a manufacturing defect.

Design Defects

In some cases, the product is manufactured correctly but is still defective because of its faulty design. One perfect example of

Foreseeability

One of the most inexact concepts in tort law is the concept of foreseeability. In many areas of tort law, the defendant's responsibility for some harm is determined by whether the harm was foreseeable. In other words, could the defendant have foreseen the harm before it happened? In a very strict sense, the answer to this question is almost always "yes."

For instance, it is entirely possible, and therefore, foreseeable, that a female motorist will find me irresistible and decide to jump from her car into mine while traveling 70 mph *in the opposite direction*. Because that event is foreseeable, do I have a legal duty to plan for it by building a "woman catcher" into my passenger door? Or should I drive on "male only" roads? The answer is obviously "no." As a legal matter, events are only foreseeable if they are reasonably likely to occur ... or if the defendant is rich.

such a product is the Jawbreaker candy from the 1970s.

As the name implies, Jawbreakers were designed to break your jaw when you bit into them. The candy was primarily sold to young children incapable of resisting the temptation to bite into the candy. As a result, the number of broken jaws and chipped teeth must have numbered in the millions.

In other cases, the law requires manufacturers to go the extra mile and build safety features into their products. One recent example of this was the introduction of the child-proof lighter. Unfortunately, the lighter has proven to be "adult-proof" as well.

Inadequate Labeling

Also, a product may be defective if it doesn't contain adequate warning labels. Many products are normally safe, but can be dangerous if used improperly (e.g., scissors, lawn mowers, spouses, etc.). As a result, the law requires manufacturers to warn consumers of dangers that may result from foreseeable *misuse* of the product.

The interesting question here is: which misuses of the product are foreseeable? Anyone who has ever seen the TV show *America's Funniest Home Videos* knows that people will do the strangest things. Therefore, a skillful lawyer can successfully argue that even the most ridiculous misuse of a product was foreseeable. This is particularly true in the case of products that fall into the hands of children, the mentally disabled or members of the House of Representatives.

Also, the warning must be understandable to the user. In many areas of the country, this requires the warning to be written in English and some other commonly spoken language. This also explains why manufacturers often use pictures as warnings, such as the skull and crossbones used to indicate poison.

Finally, in order to sue because a product lacked adequate warning labels, the danger must not be obvious. For instance, a person who sticks himself in the eye with a pencil can't sue the manufacturer for failure to warn him of the danger. If this were the case, then each product would be covered with *dozens* of warning labels. Just imagine all of the warnings that would be placed on a can of Coke:

- **Sticking your finger into the top of the can and twisting it may result in *severe* injury.**

- **Sticking *any* part of your body into the top of the can and twisting it may result in severe injury.**

- **Pouring the contents of this can into your eye will sting.**

- **Pouring the contents of this can up your nose may result in drowning.**

A *Lawpsided* View
Pop-*Torts*

In July 2001, a New Jersey woman sued Kellogg and Black & Decker for $100,000 in damages to her home caused when an unattended Pop-Tart burst into flames inside her toaster. In this case, the plaintiff put a Pop-Tart in the toaster and then drove her children to school. When she returned 20 minutes later, smoke and firemen were pouring out of her home.

It appears that, for some reason, the Pop-Tart failed to pop. The local fire department concluded that the cause of the fire was "unattended food," which is the second leading cause of domestic fires in America. The leading cause is from people who intentionally light themselves on fire to avoid watching the TV show, *Big Brother*.

Now, there was once a time in America when this would have been the end of the story. The plaintiff would have replaced the toaster and prayed that her husband didn't notice that the walls were black or that the house smelled of hickory.

However, those days are long gone in America. Instead of being defensive and embarrassed, the plaintiff took the offensive. She immediately filed a lawsuit against the manufacturers of the Pop-Tarts and the toaster.

Apparently, the lawsuit was brought under the product liability theory of *tart* law. The plaintiff claimed that both the Pop-Tarts and the toaster were defective. She claimed that the Pop-Tarts were manufactured improperly, causing them to wedge themselves into the toaster. Also, she claimed that the spring mechanism in the toaster was faulty and that it should have been designed to shut off after a certain time.

However, the plaintiff has one very large obstacle to clear in this case – the warning labels. The Pop-Tart box contains not just one, but actually two, warning labels to prevent just this situation.

The first warning label reads in bold capital letters: "ATTEND TOASTING APPLIANCE WHILE HEATING." The second warning label is in red ink and reads: "Do not leave toasting appliances unattended due to possible risk of fire." In short, she could have been warned more clearly only if the warning label read:

"Lady, don't leave these Pop-Tarts in the toaster when you take the kids to school. Also, make sure that little Katie wears her hat and gloves."

Nevertheless, the plaintiff still stands a good chance of winning a jury trial. In fact, it is entirely possible that the plaintiff's lawyer will convince the jury that Kellogg is liable because the Pop-Tart should have been designed to hurl itself out of the toaster when it reached a certain temperature. For companies like Kellogg and Black & Decker, facing a jury is riskier than betting on the white guy in a heavyweight boxing match.

- Bathing in a tub full of this product will leave you sticky.

- Eating Pop Rocks while drinking this product will kill you (like it killed "Mikey" from the *Life* cereal commercials).

Breach of Warranty

A product may also be defective if it doesn't live up to the claims made to the consumer. For instance, let's assume Lonely Larry sees an infomercial on late-night TV for the *Chick Magnet 2000*. According to the program, this revolutionary new device will make even the most pathetic loser a virtual "chick magnet." Having nothing to lose, Larry calls the 800 number and agrees to make three monthly payments at the low, low price of $69.99.

Three weeks later, the product arrives. Armed with the *Chick Magnet 2000*, Larry goes into a local bar. He approaches the most beautiful woman in the place and says, "Your place or mine?" In response, the woman punches him in the face,

knocking out most of his teeth. In this case, Larry may have a products liability claim since the product did not live up to the manufacturer's promises and as a result, Larry was injured.

Unfit for a Particular Purpose

Finally, in some cases, a product is defective even if it works for most purposes but not for the user's particular purpose. For instance, let's suppose Dim-witted Dan is driving along the highway one night when he runs out of gas. He walks into a convenience store and purchases a jar of *petroleum* jelly. He explains to the cashier that he has just run out of gas and asks if one jar will be

---

Other Common Misuses of Products

- Using the garage of your new house to store all of the junk that you didn't want at your old house

- Using your teeth on beer bottles, cans and your opponent in a sporting event

- Drinking a milkshake too fast and getting "brain freeze"

---

enough to get him home. After running into the supply room to laugh hysterically, the cashier suggests he purchase another jar, *just in case.*

Dan agrees, walks back to his car and *spoons* both jars into his gas tank. Of course, his car is severely damaged and he spends thousands of dollars in repairs (the repair guys at the garage are still enjoying a good laugh, too). In this case, Dan may sue the convenience store because the cashier *knew* that the product was not fit for the purpose for which it was being used.

WHO CAN BE SUED

One of the best things about product liability law is that it allows you to sue just about anyone. Not only can you sue the manufacturer, but you can usually also sue anyone in the supply chain – distributors, wholesalers, retailers, etc.

However, this is not always the case. For instance, you can't sue a supplier if it is not in the business of selling the product. Therefore, if you buy your Uncle Pete's car, you can't sue him under products liability if the car turns out to be defective.

Also, in order to sue a supplier, the product must have been defective when it left the supplier's hands. If the product is later made defective by others, then previous suppliers are not liable.

For instance, let's take the case of the Wrong Brothers. In the early 1800s, the Wrong Brothers

tried to create a flying machine. They bought a bicycle and attached hundreds of butterflies to it. They then rode it over a cliff, hoping to take flight.

Needless to say, this experiment ended in tragedy. Nevertheless, the Wrong Brothers could not have sued the bike manufacturer under products liability law because they modified the bike after purchasing it.

Chapter in Review
Products Liability

1. Which tort theory allows you to sue for injuries caused by a defective product?

   a.   Strict Liability

   b.   Products Liability

   c.   The theory that a jury will fall for anything

2. Who can sue under products liability?

   a.   Anybody

   b.   Everybody

   c.   All of the above

Chapter 10

VICARIOUS LIABILITY
When You Really Are Your Brother's Keeper

In tort law, you aren't only responsible for our own behavior, but in some cases, you are responsible for the behavior of others as well. This is called *vicarious liability*. Fortunately, it is only applied in limited situations.

EMPLOYER LIABILITY

Generally, an employer is vicariously liable for any harm done by its employees *during the scope of their employment*. Often the dispute in these types of cases is whether the employee was acting within the scope of her duties.

For instance, let's suppose you are shopping in Home Depot and an employee accidentally runs over your foot with a forklift. In this case, Home Depot is obviously responsible for your injuries.

However, let's suppose that instead of accidentally running over your foot, the employee gets your phone number from the sales slip and makes obscene calls to your home. In this case, Home Depot may not be liable for the employee's actions because they were outside the scope of his employment. However, in this case, Home Depot may be liable under the theory of negligent entrustment.

NEGLIGENT ENTRUSTMENT

If Home Depot *negligently entrusted* the employee with customer information, then Home Depot may be vicariously liable for his actions. For instance, if the employee was a card-carrying member of Obscene Callers Anonymous, then Home Depot was negligent in allowing him access to customer records.

The same principle applies to entrusting property. For instance, if I entrust my car to my 6-year old son, then I will be liable for the damage he causes on the road. The same is true if I entrust my car to a person who is obviously drunk, or a Kennedy.

Chapter in Review
Vicarious Liability

1. An employer is vicariously liable for a tort caused by its employee if:

   a. The employee does not apologize to the victim

   b. The employee is highly paid

   c. The employee was acting within the scope of employment

Chapter 11

DAMAGES
"Show Me the Money!"

The final chapter of this discussion of torts brings us to the issue of damages (i.e., how much you get paid). A successful plaintiff in a tort case can expect to receive the following types of damages:

- **Compensatory Damages**;
- **Punitive Damages**; and
- **Nominal Damages**.

COMPENSATORY DAMAGES

In theory, compensatory damages are awarded to *compensate* the plaintiff for the harm suffered by her. However, in some cases, no amount of money can adequately compensate the plaintiff. For instance, how much money is enough to compensate a mother for the loss of her child? Nevertheless, juries are asked to make their best guess in these matters. Of course, juries are given a lot of "help" by the lawyers for both sides.

In personal injury cases, the plaintiff is entitled to economic and non-economic damages.

Economic Damages

Economic damages compensate the plaintiff for the monetary costs of his injuries, such as medical bills, property damage and the loss of future income. Obviously, calculating medical costs is straightforward. The same is true for lost or damaged property.

If the plaintiff's property is completely destroyed, then he is entitled to receive its fair market value. If the property is simply damaged, then he is entitled to receive the cost for repair. However, this is not the case if the cost of repair exceeds the value of the property. In that case, the plaintiff will simply receive the market value of the property prior to its damage.

On the other hand, calculating the loss of a plaintiff's future earnings can be harder than one of my wife's biscuits. The law requires the jury to choose a single lump-sum amount to represent the plaintiff's lifetime future earnings.

Needless to say, this isn't an easy calculation. Moreover, if you've ever been to a restaurant when the cash register wasn't working, you know that calculating is not the strong suit of most Americans.

For instance, jury deliberations in tobacco cases often sound like this:

Jury Foreman: "OK, its time to determine the damages."

Juror #1: "I suggest that we make them pay $1 million for every cigarette in a pack."

Jury Foreman: "OK, well if there are 20 cigarettes in pack, then the amount should be ... hey, who here went to college?"

Juror #8: "I went to junior college for about three hours one day."

Jury Foreman: "Well, you'll have to do."

Juror #8: "Let's see ... 2 times 1, carry the 4, times the remainder ... that gives us $145 billion."

Jury Foreman: "Sounds right to me! Let's tell the judge that we've reached a verdict."

And the difficulty of this calculation is magnified when dealing with very young plaintiffs or plaintiffs in non-traditional fields, such as entertainment.

For instance, let's suppose Rocking Ricky is tragically injured while playing his *electric* guitar in the bathtub. He sues the guitar maker claiming that a warning label should have been placed on the guitar instructing him not to play while sitting in water. Let's further suppose he brings this suit in California, and, as a result, he wins.

The jury now has to decide how much to award Ricky in economic damages. At the time of the accident, Ricky was in a band called "Too Poor." The band was just starting out and had not yet received its "big break." It is unknown whether it would have ever received such a break. Nevertheless, the jury must decide whether Ricky should get the millions he would have earned as a member of a rock group like The Rolling Stones or whether he should receive the career earnings of the average garage band, $4.95.

Non-Economic Damages

Non-economic damages are awarded to compensate the plaintiff for pain and suffering, mental anguish and decreased quality of life. Not surprisingly, here is where the real money is in tort law.

As you know, economic damages may allow you to receive your entire lifetime earnings in a verdict. However, for most of us, this amount will just cover cab fare from the courthouse. However, regardless of your financial status, non-economic damages can run into the millions.

For instance, let's suppose Curious Carl is taking a tour of the White House. While walking down a corridor, he notices that a door to one of the rooms is ajar. Being curious, Carl pushes open the door to find Barbara Bush getting dressed. Needless to say, Carl immediately loses consciousness.

Although Carl was not hurt in the fall, he remains traumatized by what he saw. In his lawsuit against the federal government, Carl can claim that his pain and suffering and mental anguish are worth *billions* (I'd have to agree with him on this point).

Also, with non-economic damages, you may collect if your injuries have decreased the quality of your life. For instance, let's suppose Tone-deaf Tony, an avid (but terrible) singer, decides to record himself singing in the shower one morning. After hearing his voice for the first time, he becomes traumatized and can no longer bring himself to sing. Nevertheless, after reading this book, Tony brings a lawsuit against the manufacturer of the recorder. Although Tony has not suffered any physical harm, he may still claim that he has suffered a decrease in the quality of his life.

Limitations

Finally, compensatory damages may not be awarded in two situations. First, the plaintiff may not recover damages to compensate for the threat of a future harm. Compensatory damages may only be only awarded to compensate for a *specific* harm actually suffered by the plaintiff.

For instance, let's suppose your ex-girlfriend, Voodoo Vicky, casts a voodoo spell to inflict seven years of bad luck upon you. Although her actions could be thought of as an intentional tort, you can't recover compensatory damages since it is uncertain whether you will ever receive bad luck, unless, of

course, you marry her.

The second limitation of compensatory damages is that the plaintiff has a duty to mitigate, or reduce, the harm. For instance, let's suppose Manly Mike is injured by the negligence of another person. Unfortunately, Mike is far too manly to actually seek medical attention, so his injury worsens. As a result, Mike won't be able to recover for those damages that he could have avoided by seeking prompt medical attention.

PUNITIVE DAMAGES

Punitive damages are awarded in cases where the tort was willful, malicious or extremely reckless. As the name implies, the purpose of punitive damages is to punish the defendant.

Interestingly, punitive damages are not calculated according to a formula (e.g., three times compensatory damages). Instead, jurors are free to decide the proper amount of financial punishment. Because the defendant has often done something terrible to merit punitive damages, the amounts can be quite staggering.

For instance, in one case, a Florida jury assessed $145 *billion* in punitive damages against the tobacco companies. Of course, it is difficult to truly grasp the magnitude of a number as large as 145 billion. However, I can put this number in perspective for you.

If you were to add the weight of all 10 million daily viewers of *The Jerry Springer Show* (assuming an average weight of 300 lbs. each – and I'm being kind in this estimate), they would only equal 3 billion pounds. To reach 145 billion pounds, you would have to add Ricki Lake's audience as well.

Fortunately, many states allow judges to reduce punitive awards so they more accurately reflect the proper "punishment" for the defendant. In reaching this reduced amount, judges take into account the degree of harm done to the plaintiff, the wealth of the defendant, and the nature of his actions.

NOMINAL DAMAGES

Nominal damages are awarded to the plaintiff in cases where the jury would like to indicate the plaintiff has been wronged, but there has been little or no actual harm. For instance, let's suppose Bill Fences was fired from his job at Burgerland because one of his co-workers told the manager that Bill has cooties.

After being fired, Bill starts his own computer software company (which does not discriminate against people with cooties) and makes billions of dollars. Nevertheless, Bill brings a lawsuit against his former co-worker for slander. If Bill wins his lawsuit, he will probably receive just $1 in nominal damages because getting fired from Burgerland was the best thing that ever happened to him.

However, the real value of a nominal damages award is that it paves the way for punitive damages. For instance, let's suppose you see O.J. Simpson at McDonald's (after the verdict in the civil suit, this is all that he can afford). O.J. is in a surly mood so he sticks his tongue out at you. You are highly offended and bring a lawsuit against him for intentional infliction of emotional distress.

If you win the lawsuit, you will only receive nominal damages since your injuries were not severe. However, the award of nominal damages will allow the jury to impose punitive damages of $47 billion against O.J. Of course, your chances of collecting on this verdict are about as good as O.J.'s chances of finding the "real killer" on a golf course.

Chapter in Review
Damages

1. What is the purpose of compensatory damages?

    a.   To make lawyers rich

    b.   To compensate the victim for harm suffered

    c.   All of the above

2. What is the purpose of punitive damages?

    a.   To make lawyers *really* rich

    b.   To punish the defendant for wrongful behavior

    c.   All of the above

3. To determine a person's expected future earnings, you would need to know her:

    a.   Phone number

    b.   Occupation

    c.   Ethnicity

REAL PROPERTY

JUST IN CASE YOU EVER SCRAPE UP THE DOWN PAYMENT

REAL PROPERTY
OVERVIEW

Real estate law is a fundamental element of every law school curriculum. And the reason for this is as simple as Dan Quayle; every family, business, school, church or group must congregate on a plot of land *somewhere*. Therefore, understanding your rights with respect to real estate is essential.

In the next four chapters, we will discuss real property law in detail. However, please note that I will not teach you how to get a 2% mortgage with no payments until after the first year. Nor will I teach you how to make a fortune buying real estate with no money down. After all, if I knew how to do those things, I wouldn't have had to write this entire book.

Instead, we will discuss the legal fundamentals of renting (or leasing) property; what to look for in a lease; what to look *out* for in a lease; and your rights as a tenant under a lease. We will also discuss the forms of real estate ownership and how property is lawfully acquired under our legal system. Lastly, we will discuss the duties and obligations of property ownership.

Chapter 12

RENTING THE PROPERTY
Making Someone Else Rich

For most of us, our first experience with a significant contract occurred when renting our first apartment. After spending weeks finding the "perfect place" (i.e., the nicest dump you could afford), you were presented with the *lease*. This document determined the relationship between you, the *tenant*, and the owner of the property, the *landlord*, or slumlord (depending upon how much of a dump you could afford).

THE RENT

In most cases, the most important part of the lease is the amount of the rent. Usually, the rent is clearly stated in the lease (e.g., $800 per month). However, what happens if the rent isn't stated in the lease? Do you get to live in the apartment for free?

Of course not! Unless, of course, you are renting from your parents, your in-laws or someone who thinks you are *really* cute. Otherwise, you must pay the *fair market rent*, which

is the price paid for similar apartments in your immediate area.

Of course, your obligation to pay rent is contingent upon the property being available to rent. For instance, let's suppose you sign a lease to rent an apartment at the Shady Pines Retirement Center beginning next month. Currently, the apartment is occupied by Elderly Edna, who is expected to create a "vacancy" any day now. However, Edna refuses to go gently into that good night. As a result, your apartment is occupied when your lease period begins.

Remarkably, in the past, you would have been required to pay rent even though you couldn't move into the apartment. Also, you would have been responsible for evicting poor old Edna.

Fortunately, this is no longer the case. Nowadays, you will be excused from paying rent until the apartment is vacant and the

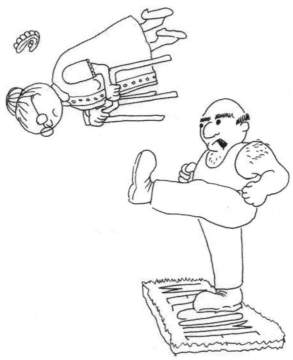

the landlord must throw poor old Edna out into the street, which for many landlords is the most satisfying part of the job.

Also, you will be excused from paying rent if your apartment building is destroyed by fire, earthquake or my brother-in-law moving into it.

THE TERM

The second most important component of a lease is the *term*. The term indicates just how long you will be obligated to pay $1,500 a month for that tiny, rat-infested dump. There are four basic terms of a lease.

Periodic Tenancy

The most common term for a residential lease is *month-to-month*. In a month-to-month lease, the tenant pays rent each month until either party terminates the lease. Of course, the terminating party must usually give some notice to the other party (usually one month's notice). This type of lease is called a *periodic tenancy*.

In most states, periodic

tenancies are the default. In other words, if no lease term is specified, then the lease is assumed to be a periodic tenancy. The length of the period is usually tied to the frequency of payments.

Therefore, if the tenant pays rent on the first of every month, then the term is assumed to be month-to-month. Likewise, if the tenant pays rent each Friday, then the term is assumed to be week-to-week. On the other hand, if the tenant hasn't paid rent since Vanilla Ice's last hit record, then the tenant is assumed to be my ex-roommate.

Annual Tenancy

Another common type of term is a *year-to-year* lease. The major difference between a month-to-month lease and a year-to-year lease is that the year-to-year lease doesn't automatically renew at the end of the year. When the year is up, you are expected to either move out or sign a new lease, usually with a higher rent.

However, what happens if the tenant wants to move out before the end of the

year? For instance, let's suppose Geeky Greg meets the woman of his dreams, Desperate Debby, on the Internet. Debby lives in another state so Greg decides to relocate to be with her. Unfortunately, the lease on Greg's apartment doesn't expire for another six months. In this case, Geeky Greg has a problem.

Unless Greg can get his landlord to let him out of the lease, he will have to pay the last six months of rent, even if he moves out. In fact, in many states, the landlord wouldn't even have to try to find a new tenant to offset the rent. The two lessons to be learned here are: (1) read the lease *carefully* to determine what happens if you terminate early and (2) don't meet women over the Internet. Actually, this second lesson applies to all areas of life.

Tenancy at Will

Another term is *tenancy at will*. Usually, this type of term is established in very informal circumstances. For instance, let's suppose Nomadic Norman convinces his rich uncle to let him crash at one of his many houses from time to time. In this case, neither Norman nor his uncle wants to be tied down to a long-term lease. Norman wants to be free to roam and his uncle wants to be free to kick Norman out when he starts using the place as a commune.

Tenancy at Sufferance

In some cases, a tenant will stay in the property past the term of the lease. This is called "tenancy at sufferance." This shouldn't be confused with "tenancy at *suffering*." This occurs when your sister, her husband and their five kids move into your home for "a few weeks" until their new home is ready and one year later, they are still there!

In dealing with a *hold-over tenant*, the landlord has two options: (1) evict the tenant or (2) assume a new periodic tenancy. Tenancies at sufferance are fairly common at the end of annual leases. In most cases, the landlord has announced a rent increase for the new term. The tenant decides to move out but can't find a new place in

---

Other Types of Periodic Tenancies

1. **Day-to-Day:** This is the term for your stay at a motel

2. **Hour-to-Hour:** This is the term for your stay at a *sleazy* motel

3. **Breath-to-Breath:** This is the term for your stay in a rest home

4. **Turn-to-Turn:** This is the term for your stay at Park Place or Boardwalk in the board game *Monopoly*

time. As a result, the tenant will usually hold-over for a month or two. In this case, the tenant must pay the new, higher rent during this hold-over period.

ASSIGNMENTS AND SUBLEASES

In some cases, you may avoid "breaking" the lease by assigning your interest in the lease or subletting the property. In an assignment, the new tenant takes your place under the existing lease. As a result, you no longer have any rights or responsibilities with respect to the property.

On the other hand, in a sublease, you remain liable to pay rent to the landlord under the original lease and your subtenant agrees to pay you rent in turn. As a result, under a sublease, you must still pay the landlord regardless of whether your subtenant actually pays you.

Nevertheless, there are some situations when a sublease is preferable to an assignment. For example, let's suppose Independent Ivan, a college student, leases an off-campus apartment in January. Ivan agrees to pay $500 per month for one year, even though he will be spending the summer at home with his parents. Obviously, Ivan wants to find a way to avoid paying rent for the three months in the summer.

Luckily, he meets Stupid Steven, who needs to make up courses at summer school. If Ivan *assigns* his lease to Steven in June, then Ivan will have to move back into the dorms in September because he will have given up all rights to the apartment. However, if Ivan sublets his apartment to Steven for three months, then Ivan can move back into the apartment in September.

Also, under this sublease, Ivan can charge more than $500 per month to Steven. After all, Economics 101 is one of the courses that Steven will be repeating during the summer. Of course, it must be remembered that Ivan is responsible for paying the rent to the landlord, regardless of whether Steven ever pays him.

Finally, please note that most real estate leases contain restrictions against assignments and subleases. Generally, the landlord must agree *in advance* to an assignment. In part, this is to protect the landlord against unnecessary credit risks. Therefore, if Bill Gates tries to assign his lease to M.C. Hammer, the landlord can say, "You can't touch this!"

In addition, most leases restrict the tenant's ability to sublease the property. On the one hand, this doesn't seem necessary because there is no credit risk for the landlord in a sublease. However, there is a risk that the new tenant will be otherwise undesirable (e.g., dirty, noisy, Republican, etc.). Also, this restriction prevents the tenant from making a windfall profit on the sublease.

For instance, let's suppose you rent a studio apartment in New York City for *$60,000* per month. Unexpectedly, Madonna moves into the penthouse suite across the street. As luck would have it, you have a perfect view into her bedroom. The paparazzi are now willing to pay you *$600,000* per month so that they can take pictures

of Madonna breastfeeding her baby (or anyone else for that matter).

In this case, your landlord is going to want some of your $540,000 per month windfall. Therefore, your landlord will probably refuse to give his consent to the sublease unless you agree to either split the profits with him or at least allow him to use your apartment from time to time for peeping purposes.

REPAIRS

In most states, unless

the lease states otherwise, the *tenant* is responsible for making repairs to the property. In fact, the tenant has a *duty* to make repairs in some cases.

For instance, let's suppose Waterlogged Wendy rents a house where the roof leaks worse than a 1976 Ford Pinto. Although Wendy loves the feeling of raindrops on her head, she has a duty to fix the leaky roof. If she doesn't, then she may have to pay the landlord for additional water damage caused by the leaky roof.

However, this isn't the case in all states. A growing minority of states require the landlord to make certain repairs. And if these repairs aren't made, the tenant has the right to:

(1) terminate the lease,

(2) stop paying rent, or

(3) make the repairs himself.

If the tenant makes the repairs, he can offset the cost of repairs against the rent.

Of course, all of this assumes that the tenant isn't responsible for the damage in the first place. There-fore, if you and your roommate destroy your apartment in an attempt to re-enact the 1986 World Series, the landlord is not responsible for repairing the damage.

Finally, the landlord is generally responsible for repairing common areas. Therefore, if the elevator in your apartment building breaks down, you need not risk your life by climbing into the elevator shaft to fix it. Besides, if you are anything like me, you really could use the exercise of walking up and down the stairs anyway.

IMPROVEMENTS

In some cases, the tenant will make improvements to the property. This is more common in commercial leases but occurs in residential leases as well. In this event, who gets to keep the improvements at the end of the lease?

As a general rule, the tenant is free to take any improvements with her so long as she repairs the damage done by removing them. Therefore, if you install a garage door opener, you can take it with you at the end of the lease so long as you repair the damage caused removing it.

However, there are limitations to this rule. If you add a room onto the house, you obviously can't take it with you. Likewise, you can't take the wallpaper with you, unless, of course, you put up that ugly wood paneling from the 1970s. In that case, your landlord will *insist* you take it with you.

DEPOSITS

Many leases require the tenant to pay some money up front. In some cases, this amount will be characterized as a "security deposit." As the name implies, the purpose of a security deposit is to give the landlord some security in the event the tenant skips out on the lease or damages the property. Of course, if you pay the rent and keep the property in good shape (i.e., you live with your girlfriend *elsewhere*), at the end of the term, you will be entitled to a refund of the security deposit *with interest* (about $2.50 at today's rates).

Please note that there is another form of deposit that you should try to avoid as if it were a call to jury duty. This is called "bonus rent." Bonus rent is usually required when you find a rent-controlled *eight-bedroom* Manhattan apartment with Central Park views for *$32/month.* In this case, the landlord will require a bonus rent payment of $32 *million* to compensate for your extremely cheap rent. The important thing to remember with bonus rent is that you *never* get it back.

EVICTION

If the tenant fails to pay rent or observe some other term of the lease, the landlord may seek an eviction. Of course, in most states, the landlord can't simply show up at your apartment with two very large men and start flinging your belongings into the street. Besides, if your children are anything like mine, your belongings have already been thrown into the street.

In court, you may assert a few defenses to eviction. As discussed above, you can claim that you haven't paid your rent because the landlord failed to make repairs. You can also claim that you are the victim of a constructive eviction.

Constructive Eviction

Under the doctrine of *constructive eviction,* you need not pay rent if your enjoyment of the property is *substantially interfered* with by the *landlord.* Common examples are excessive heat, excessive cold and excessive spouse. Therefore, if your apartment reaches temperatures of 10° below in the winter and 200° in the summer, then either you are being constructively evicted or you live in my first apartment.

However, there are two very important conditions to this doctrine. The first condition is that you must move out of the apartment to prove substantial interference. This prevents deadbeat tenants from claiming constructive eviction just to avoid paying the rent.

The second condition is that the landlord must cause the substantial interference. For instance, if your apartment is excessively cold because the thermostat is older than Dick Clark, then you have a claim for constructive eviction.

On the other hand, if your apartment is cold because your husband is too cheap to pay for heat in the winter, then you must continue paying rent. In this case, your landlord is not responsible for the excessive cold. After all, you married the cheap S.O.B.

Retaliatory Eviction

In other cases, the tenant can claim that the eviction is a *retaliatory eviction*. A retaliatory eviction occurs when the landlord retaliates against the tenant for exercising his *legal rights* under the lease. For instance, let's suppose Tattling Tommy reports the landlord's fire and safety code violations to the authorities. In this situation, the landlord, Firetrap Freddy, can't evict Tommy for this reason. However, Freddy can evict Tommy for other retaliatory reasons, such as failing to pay rent, making excessive noise or sleeping with Mrs. Freddy.

Chapter in Review
Renting the Property

1. Which of these people is a tenant at will?

    a.   Grace

    b.   A probate lawyer

    c.   A tenant who may either leave or be kicked out at will

2. You can claim constructive eviction if:

    a.   Your apartment building is currently under construction

    b.   The landlord interferes with your enjoyment of the property

    c.   You were evicted in a constructive manner

3. In an assignment, who is responsible for paying rent under the original lease?

    a.   The new tenant

    b.   The original tenant

    c.   The friend who always needs a place to "crash"

Chapter 13

REAL PROPERTY INTERESTS
Fees, Fees and More Fees

In this chapter, we will discuss the various ownership interests you can acquire in real estate.

OWNERSHIP INTERESTS

The Fee Simple

The *fee simple* is the most common form of property ownership in America. In short, a fee simple interest gives the owner *complete* ownership of the property. The fee simple owner is free to use the property in any lawful manner. Also, she is free to sell or give away the property.

Fee simple ownership is what most of us envision when we think of property ownership. However, this wasn't always the case. In the past, it was quite common to have less than total ownership of real estate.

The Life Estate

As the name implies, a *life estate* gives the owner an interest in the property during his lifetime. At first glance, this seems just like a fee simple because no man can own property after death (or divorce for that matter).

Nevertheless, a life estate is substantially different from a fee simple. For instance, let's assume Uncle Moneybags gives your dear old mother a life estate in a house in Malibu. As an only child, you will inherit all of your mother's property upon her death. If your mother owned the house in *fee simple*, you would have the normal incentive to stuff her with fatty foods, cigarettes and alcohol so you could inherit the house sooner. However, in the case of a life estate, the house will go back to Uncle Moneybags upon her death. As a result, you won't receive a financial reward for mistreating your mother. On the other hand, sometimes the reward is in the doing.

NOTE FROM THE AUTHOR: Momma, you know that I'm kidding, right? I love you very much. By the way, did you

get that carton of cigarettes, case of gin and box of Bon Bons I sent you for Mother's Day?

Also, a life estate limits your right to use the property because you must maintain it for the future owner. For instance, the life estate owner must keep the property in good repair and pay the mortgage and property taxes. Also, she can't use up all the property's natural resources, leaving nothing for the future owner.

For instance, let's suppose that Hillbilly Hillary has a life estate on a large plot of land. If Hillary strikes oil one day, she can't sell the rights to Exxon and move to Beverly Hills with her kinfolk, the Clampetts. Hillary must preserve the oil for the future owners. However, Hillary will be entitled to use enough of the oil to meet her daily needs for cooking, heating and brewing moonshine.

Historically, the primary purpose of the life estate was to allow a man to provide a home for his widow and to ensure the property passed on to his children. For instance, let's take the example of Conscientious

Carl and Disloyal Doris. Upon his death, Carl would like for Doris to be able to live in the house until her death, at which time, the house will belong to their children.

However, if Carl simply leaves the property to Doris in *fee simple*, his kids may receive nothing. For instance, let's suppose Doris remarries a much younger man, Gigolo Gerry. A few

years later, Doris dies (but with a smile on her face) and leaves *all* her possessions to Gerry. In this case, Carl's children will not have smiles on their faces because they will get *nothing*.

On the other hand, let's suppose Carl leaves Doris a life estate in the property. Upon her death, the house then passes to his children. In this case, Gerry better

marry for love.

Variations of the Fee Simple

There are some situations in which the owner of the property (the *grantor*) wishes to transfer ownership but only on certain conditions. For instance, let's suppose Little Orphan Annie grows up to be a very homely woman. As a result, Daddy Warbucks becomes desperate to get her out of the house, as many of the plants are beginning to wilt. Daddy Warbucks finds a man with limited means (and even more limited eyesight) and offers to buy the man a house if he marries Annie. However, to prevent the man from immediately divorcing Annie after receiving the house, Daddy Warbucks puts the following language into the transfer documents:

"I hereby deed the property to Mr. Magoo so long as he does not divorce Annie."

If Mr. Magoo divorces Annie, the property will automatically revert back to Daddy Warbucks. On the other hand, if Mr. Magoo remains married to Annie for life, then the property will be passed on to his heirs.

In some situations, a person other than the grantor is chosen to get the property if the grantee fails to live up to the condition. For instance, let's suppose Insecure Isaac dies leaving one son, Ungrateful Eugene. In Isaac's will, he gives his mansion, Isaac Manor, to Eugene so long as Eugene does not rename it.

In this scenario, Isaac must name a back-up beneficiary if he wants his restriction to have any effect. For instance, let's suppose Isaac doesn't name a back-up beneficiary. If Eugene renames the mansion "Not Isaac's Manor," then Eugene loses the property. However, the property will immediately pass to Isaac's heir, which may very well be Eugene.

However, let's suppose Isaac names The United Way as a back-up beneficiary. In this case, if Eugene renames the mansion, then ownership will pass to The United Way. By naming a back-up beneficiary, Isaac can prevent Eugene from renaming the mansion. Of course, Isaac won't be able

to prevent United Way executives from spending his donation on limousine rides, expensive hotel rooms and even more expensive escorts.

Executory Interests

As a technical matter, the person named as the backup owner has an ownership interest in the property. For instance, let's suppose Whiskey William scribbles out the following note one night:

"I hereby deed my house located on Elm Street, number 251 ... 125 ... the red one damnit, to my son, Tommy ... Tony ... the tall one, damnit. However, if Tommy ever runs out of Jack Daniels when I come to visit then he can get out and my other son, Ja ... the short one, can have it."

In this case, "the short one" has an *executory interest* in the house. However, this *executory interest* isn't worth much. After all, "the short one" would have a difficult time getting a second mortgage on his "executory interest." In fact, if his credit is anything like mine, he's going to have a hard time getting *any* kind of loan.

CONCURRENT ESTATES

In many cases, two or more people will own property together. Despite *owning* the property, each joint owner is referred to as a "tenant." In this situation, each tenant's rights are largely determined by the type of tenancy.

Joint Tenancy

Usually, husbands and wives hold property in *joint tenancy.* Each spouse holds an equal interest in the property. In many states, each spouse is free to transfer his or her share of the property to another person.

However, in community property states like California, spouses hold property in a *tenancy by the entirety.* This differs from a joint tenancy in that neither spouse may sell or mortgage any part of the property without the consent of the other party. Of course, in reality, it would be very difficult to mortgage *half* of

a house anyway. Imagine the difficulties the lender would face foreclosing on just the kitchen, the den and one of the bedrooms.

As an example, let's suppose two older, swinging widowers, Liver-spotted Larry and Gum-flapping Gary, buy a house together as "joint tenants." If Larry

dies first, then none of his heirs will share in the property because Gary will own the property all by himself.

In joint tenancies and

tenancies by the entirety, if one tenant dies, the surviving tenant becomes the owner of the entire property. This is called "the right of survivorship." This is much like the TV show, *Survivor*, except that you don't have to eat bugs. Of course, if your spouse cooks like mine, then maybe eating bugs isn't all that bad.

To avoid this unfair result, many states won't assume that a joint tenancy has been created unless the deed specifically states that the owners are "joint tenants with right of survivorship."

Tenancy in Common

In the case of Larry and Gary, a better arrangement would be for them to own the property as *tenants in common*. Tenants in common can pass their separate interests along to their heirs. Therefore, if Larry dies first, his children and grandchildren will have right to move into the house with Gary (lucky Gary!).

Also, a tenant in common may sell his interest to a third party. For instance,

let's suppose Larry doesn't die but instead becomes irritated with Gary for leaving his false teeth all over the house. One morning, after finding Gary's false teeth in his oatmeal, Larry decides to get even by selling his share of the house to Weakbladdered Wendell (a/k/a Whizzing Wendell). Unfortunately for Gary, Larry is legally entitled to do so.

As the new tenant in common, Wendell will be allowed access to all parts of the house. Therefore, Gary can't establish a "No Pee Zone" by simply drawing a line down the middle of the house and confining Wendell to the smelly part.

However, if Gary can find a sympathetic judge, he may be able to have his interest *partitioned* from Wendell's. In this event, Gary will be allowed to sell the house and split the money with Wendell. In the case of a large estate, a judge may partition the land by drawing a line down the middle of the estate and giving each tenant complete ownership of one-half of the property.

Also, as tenants in common, Gary and Wendell will share in the costs of all repairs, improvements, taxes, mortgages and fumigations. Likewise, they will share in all profits from the property.

For instance, let's suppose they supplement their incomes by giving tours of Wendell's room to people suffering from *serious* nasal congestion. In this case, Gary will be entitled to half of the profits even though Wendell is supplying 90% of the pee. As they say, "ownership does have its privileges."

Chapter in Review
Real Property Interests

1. What is a fee simple interest in real property?
   a. An interest owned after paying a simple fee
   b. Forrest Gump's closing fees
   c. Complete ownership of the property

2. What is an executory interest?
   a. A possible future ownership interest
   b. A current ownership interest
   c. The repossession of your home by a bank vice president

3. Which of the following tenancies does NOT allow for the right of survivorship?
   a. Joint tenancy
   b. Tenancy in common
   c. Marriage

Chapter 14

ACQUIRING REAL ESTATE
No Good Deed Goes Unlitigated

If you ever finally manage to scrape up a down payment (i.e., you borrow the money from mommy and daddy), you can become a homeowner. At this point, you may decide to take your first big step into the world of real estate by contacting a realtor.

THE REALTOR

A realtor, or real estate agent, is the person who introduces you to the seller of the property. Realtors are licensed real estate professionals with years of specific training in all aspects of real property. This training allows them to provide professional insights, such as "this is the kitchen – you can cook in here!" And the best part is that they only charge a 6% commission for their "expertise."

However, the important thing to remember is that the realtor works for the seller. The seller pays the realtor's commission and therefore, her first duty is to the seller and not the buyer. Therefore, buyers must remember that no matter how many times the realtor says, "you look just like my niece" or "you are such a 'handsome couple,'" she is not on your side.

In fact, because of the commission structure, the realtor's incentive is to obtain the highest possible price for the house. For instance, let's suppose Gabby Glenda, the realtor, signs a listing agreement to sell a house in worse shape than Marlon Brando, only smaller. If Gabby sells the house to John Q. Homebuyer for $50,000, she will earn a $3,000 commission. However, if Glenda can sell the house to Helen Keller for $100,000, she will double her commission.

In fact, this probably explains why lady realtors tend to be so heavily perfumed. As tears form in the eyes of buyers, they tend to miss tiny defects, such as leaky faucets, stained carpet or a missing roof.

Interestingly, in many real estate transactions, there are two realtors. The

first realtor is the one who obtained the listing from the seller. The second realtor is the person who actually found the buyer. However, as a buyer, you should never be confused that either of these people works for you. They both work for the seller and will split the commission between them. The buyer should also try to avoid ever being in the same room with the two realtors. The combined level of false compliments, keen observation and *perfumation* could be lethal.

DEEDS

As discussed earlier, the Statute of Frauds requires all contracts concerning real property to be in writing. In 21st century America, most buyers and sellers enter into purchase and sale agreements. These are fairly large documents, which are basically incomprehensible to everyone, including the lawyers who draft them. Moreover, at closing, you are usually presented with a stack of documents taller than your new house.

However, the contract need not be so involved. In fact, all that is legally required is a simple land contract called a "deed."

Signatures

A valid deed must be signed by the person transferring title to the property (the *grantor*). This seems fairly obvious, right? However, law school textbooks are filled with cases involving unsigned deeds. However, in fairness, most of these cases occurred at a time when the literacy rate was lower than Dan Quayle's SAT scores. As a result, getting a signature wasn't always easy. On second thought, given the current state of our public schools, the law students of tomorrow can expect many more of these cases in their textbooks.

Delivery

To be effective, the deed must also be delivered. For example, let's suppose Forgetful Freddy writes and signs a deed giving his home to his girlfriend, Easy Ethel. Not surprisingly, Freddy forgets to deliver the deed to Ethel. If Freddy dies soon thereafter, the house will belong to Freddy's heirs instead of Ethel because the deed was never delivered.

To be valid, the deed must be delivered to either: (1) the *grantee* (the person receiving the property) or (2) a third party. For instance, in the previous example, Freddy could have delivered the deed to Ethel or to his lawyer with instructions to give it to Ethel.

However, in some cases, using a third party to deliver a deed can be risky. For instance, let's suppose Freddy suspects Ethel is cheating on him (they don't call her Easy Ethel for nothing). Therefore, Freddy instructs his lawyer to visit Ethel and make a pass at her. If she rejects the pass, then the lawyer is to deliver the deed to her. On the other hand, if she accepts his advances, then the lawyer must destroy the deed.

Let's further suppose that the next day Freddy remembers that he broke up with Ethel three years ago. He calls his lawyer and instructs him to destroy the deed. However, the lawyer refuses because he is now excited about his "date" with Ethel.

That night, Ethel rejects the lawyer's advance as if he were ... well, as if he were a lawyer. He then

hands over the deed, as well as his wallet and the keys to his car.

Interestingly, in some states, Ethel would be legally entitled to the house. In these states, Freddy's delivery of the deed became effective when he gave the deed to his lawyer, regardless of his later change of heart. In other states, Freddy would be allowed to change his mind anytime before the deed was delivered to Ethel.

Acceptance

Although the grantor must sign and deliver the deed, the grantee is not required to sign it. In fact, a deed may become effective without any act of acceptance on the part of the grantee. Nevertheless, the grantee does have the right to refuse ownership of the property. Therefore, if a distant relative gives you his glowing estate in Chernobyl, you don't have to move there and raise five-legged livestock. Obviously, the same principle applies to any property located in New Jersey.

Identification

Also, to be effective, the deed must clearly identify the grantee. For example, let's suppose Desperate Daniel is trying to win the heart (and other body parts) of a pretty, young woman in a bar. To impress her, he signs over a deed to his house by writing the following note on the back of a cocktail napkin:

I hereby transfer my house to the most beautiful woman in the world!

From David's description of the grantee, every pretty woman in America could claim the house as her own. As a result, the deed is invalid.

NOTE FROM THE AUTHOR: Guys, don't even think about it! Don't attempt to use this as a pick-up line. For one, you will look like a dork, unless, of course, you live in California. In that case, signing over your home in advance is smart because it saves on attorneys' fees later. Second, you may encounter a female judge who has had this trick played on her before. In short, stick with the standard lies. They work just fine.

Also, the deed must sufficiently identify the property being transferred. In many cases, the most accurate description of a property is its description in the county recorder's office. Nevertheless, a street address is usually sufficient. Also, the property may be described by its boundaries. However, colorful colloquialisms, such as "in the boondocks", "off yonder" and "smack dab in the middle" will result in your deed being more invalid than Darryl Strawberry's driver's license.

RECORDING ACTS

To prevent sellers from selling the same property to multiple people, each state has a recording act. A recording act allows property owners to record their ownership interests with the state. As a result, subsequent purchasers can verify the rightful owner of the property.

There are three types of recording acts in use:

(1) race statutes;

(2) notice statutes; and

(3) race-notice statutes.

To illustrate, let's suppose Crooked Carl sells his home to Slow Sam on Monday. On Tuesday, he sells the same house to Quick Quinn, who immediately records his deed with the state. On Wednesday, Sam attempts to file his deed but is unable to do so because of Quinn's earlier filing. Sam then brings a lawsuit to *quiet title*, or in other words, to decide who is the rightful owner.

Race

In a state that operates under a race statute, Quinn wins because he recorded his deed first. Fortunately, only a few states encourage high-speed races to the courthouse by using this type of recording act.

Notice

Under a notice statute, the later purchaser prevails unless he had notice of the prior transfer. Therefore, if Quinn had actual notice of the sale to Sam, he would lose at trial.

The same would be true if Quinn had *constructive notice* of the sale. As a matter of law, purchasers have constructive notice of all prior recordings. Therefore, had Sam filed first, Quinn would have had constructive notice of the transfer and therefore, he would lose out to Sam.

In fact, Quinn would lose even if he just should have known about the sale to Sam. For instance, let's suppose Quinn drove by the house on Monday and saw Sam standing on the front lawn in his underwear screaming, "It's all mine, baby! All mine!" This

would have been enough to put Quinn on notice that Sam was the owner of the property (and in need of serious therapy).

Race-Notice

The last type of recording statute is the race-notice statute. This is similar to the notice statute except that the later purchaser must also record his deed first to prevail. For example, let's suppose Quinn didn't record his deed until Friday. In the meantime, Freddy files his deed. In this case, even if Quinn purchased the property without notice of Sam's transaction, Sam will prevail because he recorded first.

Are you getting a headache yet? If not, you will soon because the recording acts only apply to certain grantees, namely, people who pay for the property. Therefore, in our earlier example, if Quinn received the property as a gift after it had been *sold* to Sam, he wouldn't be entitled to the property no matter what he knew or when he recorded his deed.

Finally, the *grantor* may not rely on the recording act to void a prior sale. For instance, let's suppose you sell a home in Tupelo, Mississippi to a buyer who never records the deed. Two years later, historians discover that Elvis Presley once played in the backyard of this home. As a result, the market value of the

property skyrockets as Elvis fans pay to see "The Sandbox That Elvis Once Sat In." Even though the new owner never recorded his deed, you can't get your house back. Although if you are nice to him, he may let you have a tour of your old backyard for half price.

TITLE INSURANCE

In reality, these problems arise infrequently due to title insurance. In most cases, before purchasing a property, the buyer (or his bank) will obtain a title insurance policy from a title company. This policy insures that the buyer will obtain legal title to the property from the seller. In order to write the policy, the title company does a thorough check of the state's title records to determine the seller's legal authority to sell the property. Lastly, the title company ensures that the new deed is recorded immediately.

ADVERSE POSSESSION

Although the vast majority of home sales in America involve realtors, deeds and falsifying mortgage applications, there is another way to acquire real estate – *adverse possession*. A trespasser may acquire property by adverse possession after a certain period of time (e.g., 15 years) if the lawful owner doesn't take steps to eject him from the property. This is also referred to as "squatter's rights."

This concept goes back hundreds of years to the days when Strom Thurmond was first elected to the U.S. Senate. Its purpose is to protect people who spend years working and living on a piece of property only to discover later that the property technically belongs to someone else.

Obviously, this concept usually applies to plots of rural land where boundaries may be unclear. After all, if a stranger moves into your 200 sq. ft. studio apartment, it won't take you 30 years (or even 30 seconds) to have him removed.

The law places the burden upon the property owner to secure her property and take action against trespassers. If she fails to do so, then the law employs a "you snooze, you lose" approach.

Of course, as I've said before, nothing in the law is that simple. Nevertheless, there are three basic elements to the concept of adverse possession:

(1) The Time Element;

(2) The Mental Element; and

(3) The Physical Element.

The Time Element

In order to acquire property by adverse possession, the trespasser must occupy the property for a specified time period. In this area, state laws vary significantly. In some states, adverse possession can be established in just a few short years. In other states, adverse possession can take as long as 30 years or more.

In some cases, the required time period may be extended, or *tolled*. If the owner is unable to detect the trespasser because of some extraordinary circumstance, then the clock doesn't start running until the owner recovers. For example, if the owner is incarcerated at the time of the initial trespass, then the time period won't start until he is released. The same would be true if the property owner suffers from some other temporary condition that makes it difficult to monitor the property.

For instance, let's suppose Democratic Dan served as a delegate to the 2000 Democratic National Convention. Like most delegates, Dan was literally bored into a coma while listening to Al Gore's acceptance speech. Upon hear-

hearing the news, Dan's neighbor, Republican Ron, moves into Dan's house. In this case, the adverse possession period won't start until Dan regains consciousness. The same would be true if Dan were imprisoned, confined or in

line at *Starbucks*.

However, the adverse possession period won't be extended simply because the property owner is on vacation or living out of the state. Absent property owners are responsible for monitoring their property, even from afar.

Also, the period of trespass must be continuous. Therefore, a participant in the original Woodstock Festival can't claim ownership of the farm in upstate New York simply because he also attended the reunion concert 30 years later.

Of course, the continuous possession requirement doesn't mean that the trespasser may never leave the property. The trespasser must merely occupy the property in the same manner as an owner would. For instance, let's suppose Free-loading Freddy moves into an abandoned house in Phoenix. Like many Arizona residents, Freddy spends most of the year in another part of the country, where temperatures do not routinely exceed 100° *Celsius*. Nevertheless, after 10 years, Freddy may still claim ownership of the house by adverse possession.

The Mental Element

The second element of adverse possession is the mental element. In short, the trespasser must have a good faith belief that he is entitled to the property. Therefore, a person can't intend to *steal* property by adverse possession.

However, please note that the trespasser's belief need not be reasonable, just in good faith. For instance, let's suppose Gullible Gus "buys" the Brooklyn Bridge for $200 from a guy he meets in an alley. Gus immediately moves his possessions onto the bridge. In New York, the statutory period for adverse possession is only 10 years.

In this case, it is easily conceivable that Gus could live on the Brooklyn Bridge for 10 years as New Yorkers simply drive around (and over) him. If, after 10 years, Gus claims ownership of the bridge, his claim will not fail simply because it is idiotic.

It will fail because a trespasser must be hostile to the interests of others in the property. Of course, this "hostility" requirement doesn't mean that Gus must yell obscenities at drivers as they speed pass (that is required by a different New York law). However, Gus would have to take some action to obtain sole possession of the bridge, such as putting doors on both sides to prevent cars from traveling through his "living room."

No Trespassing Signs

People often try to satisfy the hostility requirement by posting "No Trespassing" signs on doors, fences and gates. However, this isn't necessary. After all, the fact that the owner has erected boundaries around the property is enough notice of his intent to keep the property to himself. And if a trespasser isn't deterred by a gate or a fence, then a cardboard sign isn't going to do the trick.

The Physical Element

Obviously, in addition to satisfying the time and mental elements, the trespasser must be in physical possession of the property. In addition, the trespasser's possession must be open and notorious. Therefore, you can't gain adverse possession of your neighbor's house by sneaking into his basement each night. Trust me on this one.

Chapter in Review
Acquiring Real Property

1. To satisfy the Statute of Frauds, all real estate must be transferred by:

   a. Century 21

   b. Carleton Sheets

   c. A written document

2. Under a race statute, who wins?

   a. The white guy

   b. The first person to record his interest

   c. Carl Lewis

3. Which of the following is NOT an element of adverse possession?

   a. Hydrogen

   b. Time

   c. Physical

Chapter 15

USING THE PROPERTY
Doing Unto Your Neighbor
Before He Sues Unto You

Even if you own your home free and clear, you don't have an absolute right to use the property in any manner you choose. This is particularly true if you live in a typical neighborhood, where the houses are located closer together than DNA molecules. In short, homeowners are expected to live by the golden rule – never move into the house next door to the neighbor with a gold tooth.

NUISANCE

If a property owner uses his property in a manner that *substantially* and *unreasonable interferes* with the rights of others to use their property, then he has created a nuisance.

Of course, the important thing to remember is that the interference must be substantial and unreasonable. Interference is substantial if it causes actual physical harm to people or property. For instance, let's suppose my mother hangs a pair of my father's

dirty socks on the clothesline. The smell from his socks soon permeates the entire neighborhood, causing coughing, choking and frantic calls to the local realtor. In this case, my mother has created a nuisance.

Also, interference can be substantial even if no physical harm occurs. However, this is only if the typical neighbor would find it offensive, seriously annoying or intolerable. For instance, let's suppose God-fearing Gary holds a weekly

Bible study at his home. His neighbor, Hedonistic Henry, is "disturbed" by these meetings.

Obviously, in this case, Gary has not created a nuisance because his weekly meetings are not offensive, seriously annoying or intolerable to the typical person. However, if Gary's weekly meetings start to get out of hand and the chants of "Oh God! Oh God!" become less religious in nature, then Gary has created a nuisance. Although in this case, I suspect that Henry won't mind at all.

Also, in determining whether the interference is "unreasonable," a court will examine a number of factors, including the harm caused, the nature of the locality and which party began their use first. Obviously, if you decide to build your dream house next to a nightclub, you can't complain about the traffic, the noise or the fact that the deejay insists upon playing the same song 20 times each night.

On the other hand, if Texaco builds a factory next door that spews more toxic material than the rapper Eminem, then you may have a case that the factory is a nuisance. In any event, we all have a case that Eminem is a nuisance.

NOTE FROM THE PUBLISHER: We would like to apologize to Eminem on behalf of the author. More importantly, we'd like to remind Mr. Nem that publishers are not responsible for the work of their authors. Therefore, if someone needs to "have a cap busted off in them," it is the author and not us.

SUPPORT RIGHTS

Needless to say, property owners may not take actions that remove the underground support from their neighbor's land. For instance, let's suppose Armageddon Aaron builds a 20,000 sq. ft. bunker under his neighborhood to prepare for the end of the world.

Unfortunately, Aaron doesn't have any experience in construction and builds the bunker using instructions he downloads from endoftheworld.com. As a result, the bunker collapses quicker than the Boston Red Sox in the playoffs.

This causes substantial damage to a number of homes in his neighborhood.

In this case, Aaron has violated his duty to provide support rights for his neighbors and therefore, is responsible for the damages.

Another example of this principle involves underground mineral rights. For instance, let's suppose Lucky Lou discovers underneath his home the largest deposit of natural gas not involving my father. Let's further suppose that he sells the underground rights in his property to the local gas company but he sells the land and the house to someone else. In this case, the gas company may extract as much natural gas as it desires so long as it does nothing to cave in the land and the house.

WATER RIGHTS

In most states, if you own property along a lake or stream, you are entitled to a "reasonable use" of the water. However, your water usage can't substantially interfere with the water rights of other property owners along the path of the lake or stream. Therefore, a person living along a stream may use the water for drinking, bathing and farming. However, he may not sell water to *Evian* if this would dry up the stream and deprive others of its use.

However, this reasonable use rule doesn't apply in the western states. In these states, legal use of lakes and streams is determined on a "first-come first-serve" basis. If a person can establish a prior use of the water, then he may continue using the water. This is the case even if he doesn't own property adjoining the water.

For instance, let's suppose Inland Irving has been using a stream for years to obtain water for the wet T-shirt contests at his night club. In this case, even if people build homes along the stream, Irving will still have the right to take water from the stream. This is the case even if his water usage leaves the homeowners with no water for drinking, cooking or bathing.

However, not only do landowners fight to get water, but they also fight to get rid of water. In some cases, a landowner's efforts to drain surface water from his property will result in flooding of a neighbor's property. Interestingly, state laws vary on this issue. There are three different approaches:

(1) The Civil Law Approach;

(2) The Common Enemy Approach; and

(3) The Reasonable Use Approach.

Civil Law

About half of the states use the *civil law* approach to water rights. Under the civil law, a property owner is required to allow water to flow in its natural course over the property. Therefore, if the landowner can't drain the water without causing flooding amongst his neighbors, then he must learn to swim.

Common Enemy

In about one-third of the states, surface waters are

treated as a *common enemy*, much like those annoying boy bands. In these states, a landowner may divert surface water from his property even if doing so will turn the rest of his neighborhood into the lost city of Atlantis.

Reasonable Use

The remaining states use a reasonable use approach. In these states, a landowner may alter the natural flow of water across her land so long as there is no substantial interference with her neighbors' use of their land. Unlike the civil law approach, the reasonable use approach allows courts to balance the interests of the competing landowners. In doing so, courts will examine the harm to be suffered by each property owner and whether alternatives exist to correct the drainage problem.

In short, the reasonable use approach allows judges to act reasonably. Obviously, this is a very new concept in the law.

AIR RIGHTS

As a technical matter, each property holder owns not only the land but also the air above her land. Therefore, a trespasser will not be excused for encroaching upon your property just because he never actually sets foot on it.

For instance, let's suppose Sunny Sally enjoys sunbathing by her pool. To protect her privacy, she erects a high wall around her home. However, her next door neighbor, Peeping Paul, is determined to "sneak a peek." Therefore, he rents a helicopter and hovers just above her backyard. In this case, Paul is not only pathetic but also, guilty of trespass.

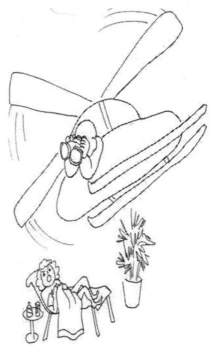

However, air rights aren't always exclusive. For instance, a commercial airliner may travel over your land at 30,000 feet without committing a trespass. This is because the airplane doesn't cause a disturbance for the homeowner, who can neither hear nor see the plane passing overhead. Obviously, the situation would be different if the same plane were to pass only 30 feet above the property.

EASEMENTS

In some cases, third parties will have a right to use the land for a specified purpose. This is called an *easement*. The perfect example of an easement is the right of your neighbors to use the sidewalk in front of your house.

Although the sidewalk is technically on your property, the public has a right to use it to cross your property. Of course, your neighbors' rights in this instance are limited to *traveling* along the sidewalk. Therefore, they can't use your sidewalk to throw parties, store their junk or park their cars. Except, of course, in my neighbor-

hood, where parking seems to be permitted everywhere but in one's own garage.

The rules concerning the creation of an easement are very technical and can only be understood after years of legal study or the deposit of a hefty retainer with my firm. For instance, easements can be created by express grant, by implication, and even, by prescription.

"Take two easements and call me in the morning."

Easements can also be created by necessity. For instance, let's suppose Deadbeat Dan is a struggling actor still living at home with his mother. Dan's mother begins to realize that Dan will never leave her house. Therefore, she *sells* his second-story bedroom to him.

Let's further assume that the transfer deed does not provide an easement for Dan to cross through his mother's portion of the house in order to get to his room. Finally, let's assume Dan and his mother get into a fight and now, she refuses to allow him to step foot in *her* part of the house.

In this case, Dan won't have to enter and exit his room by ladder because he has an easement created by necessity. This easement will allow Dan to pass through his mother's part of the house but it won't permit him to make stops at the refrigerator or even the bathroom for that matter. In short, Dan would be smart to apologize to his mother.

COVENANTS

In some cases, a seller will require the buyer to make certain promises (*covenants*) in order to complete the transaction. In this case, the question is often whether the covenant "runs with the land" or is simply a contractual matter between the buyer and the seller.

If the covenant runs with the land, then all subsequent purchasers of the property must abide by it. On the other hand, if the covenant is merely a contractual arrangement between the buyer and the seller, then subsequent purchasers are free to ignore it.

For a covenant to run with the land, it must "touch and concern" the land. In other words, the covenant must reduce the owner's use and enjoyment of the land. For instance, let's suppose Moonshine Melvin owns two adjoining parcels of land. He agrees to sell one parcel to Homebrew Herman on the condition that Herman agrees not to make his competing homebrew on the property. If Herman agrees, this covenant will run with the land and prevent the next owner, Corn Liquor Carl, from competing with Melvin as well.

On the other hand, using the previous example, let's suppose that the covenant only required Herman to help Melvin make his moonshine. In this case, the covenant will not run with the land and therefore,

Carl can devote 100% of his time to his own thriving homebrew business.

Also, the parties must intend for the covenant to run with the land. For instance, let's suppose Grandma Greta gives her favorite grandson a house on the condition that he visits every Saturday for milk and cookies. Obviously, this is a personal covenant that isn't intended to run with the land. Therefore, if the grandson sells the house, the new owner won't have to spend each Saturday hearing about how movies, cigarettes and brand new homes cost just a quarter in the "good old days."

Sadly, in the not-so-distant past, land deeds often contained restrictive covenants preventing the owner from selling to African-Americans, Jews or anyone who voted for Ross Perot in the 1996 Presidential Election. Although these covenants certainly run with the land, as a matter of public policy, judges refuse to enforce them.

ZONING

In most cities and towns, zoning laws have been enacted to regulate use of the land. These laws serve a number of different purposes.

For instance, zoning laws often segregate uses of property and thereby, prevent Exxon from putting a refinery at the end of your block.

Now, some of you are saying, "Hey, but there is an Exxon refinery on my block!" This is because cities and towns often grant exceptions (or *variances*) to prevent "unnecessary hardships," such as reductions in campaign contributions.

In addition, a *pre-existing use* will often be allowed to continue even if it violates the zoning laws so long as it doesn't create a danger to the public. For instance, let's suppose Karaoke Ken is the owner of a karaoke club. One day, his town passes a zoning ordinance requiring all karaoke clubs to be located next to schools for the deaf. In this case, Ken would probably be allowed to continue running his club at its current location because karaoke doesn't pose a danger to the public, unless, of course, I happen to be singing.

A *Lawpsided* View
Easements

The most notorious family feud in American history involved the Hatfields and the McCoys. Historical accounts of the feud differ. Some historians believe that the feud erupted after the theft of Randolph "The Real" McCoy's hog and the impregnation of his daughter. Other historians believe that it was the other way around. In any event, over a dozen years, 6 Hatfields and 6 McCoys were killed in this feud.

Despite this history, the descendants of the two families came together in the summer of 2000 for an inter-family reunion. And according to news accounts, there was not a single fight, shooting or pig theft during the 3-day event. After more than a century of feuding, the two clans seemed to be at peace.

Unfortunately, this peace is now threatened and the latest episode in this inter-family saga could prove to be the most dangerous. While the 19th century skirmishes were fought with rifles and pitchforks, the latest battles may be waged using far more lethal weapons – lawyers.

The dispute involves access to a cemetery where three McCoys are buried. John Vance, a Hatfield descendant, owns a piece of land adjoining the cemetery and is refusing to allow people to cross his land to get to the cemetery.

Joseph Justice, a lawyer and descendant of the McCoys, has sent a letter to Vance asking him to reverse his stance. If Vance doesn't acquiesce, Justice may be forced to take the next step – impregnating Vance's daughter or pig, whichever comes first.

Now, the law of real estate varies from state to state. However, there are some principles of real estate that apply in every state. These principles are borrowed from the common law tradition of England.

The common law dates back hundreds of years. At the time, it was not possible or practical to actually write out laws. So, instead, judges pretty much made things up as they went along. When asked to defend a decision, they would say, "Sir, that is just plain old common sense" (thus, the term "common law").

Under the common law, a person generally had the exclusive right to use his land and to keep out all trespassers.   However, there were some circum-stances when others would be given rights to use a landowner's property.

These rights had fancy names like easements, cove-nants and equitable servitudes. Moreover, they were subject to more qualifying conditions than a "New Car For No Money Down and 0% Interest Financing" ad on the radio.

Therefore, in an effort to simplify this analysis, let me just say that a judge might find for Vance in this case and allow him to refuse entry to the cemetery. Or the judge might find for Justice and compel Vance to let the cemetery visitors pass. It's really just a matter of common sense (see how it works!).

In general, a municipality's power to enact zoning laws is almost unlimited. So long as the ordinance is remotely reasonable, the courts will uphold it. The only exception to this rule is if the ordinance has a disproportionate impact on minorities and the poor.

For instance, some affluent communities have used zoning laws to prevent the "less desirable element" from settling in their towns. These towns require *all* homes to be as large as Rush Limbaugh's head, only less empty. Therefore, unless you can afford a 12,000 sq. ft. home, you can't live in these communities.

Finally, some communities have used even more drastic methods to keep out would-be homeowners – homeowners' associations. In these neighborhoods, each homeowner agrees to be bound by the rules of the association. The association decides such things as when Christmas lights must be taken down, which shades of off-white are acceptable as house colors and when to sue the builder for construction defects. Obviously, these are important decisions that can't be entrusted to individual homeowners, but rather should be made by trained professionals (i.e., the busy-bodies willing to serve on these boards).

Chapter in Review
Using the Property

1. In order to create a nuisance, you must:

   a.   Have unprotected sex

   b.   Cause a substantial and unreasonable interference with a neighbor's property

   c.   Invite my brother-in-law to spend the weekend

2. A covenant is enforceable against a future landowner if it:

   a.   Runs with the land

   b.   Walks with the land

   c.   Drives ahead and waits for the land

3. Which of the following are not rights enjoyed by landowners?

   a.   Air rights

   b.   Water rights

   c.   Fire rights

CONSTITUTIONAL LAW

CAN WE REALLY TRUST A DOCUMENT WRITTEN BY MEN WEARING TIGHTS, WIGS AND MAKE-UP?

CONSTITUTIONAL LAW
OVERVIEW

In the summer of 2002, we celebrated the 215th birthday of the U.S. Constitution. At 215 years old and counting, our Constitution is the oldest living document in the world today, with the possible exception of Strom Thurmond's diary.

In truth, this document, and the philosophy it embodies, is largely responsible for our success as a nation. Over the years, *millions* of people have come to America in pursuit of the freedoms guaranteed by this grand document – the freedom of speech, the freedom of religion, the freedom to file frivolous lawsuits, etc.

Of course, the Constitution is by no means a perfect document. In fact, with regards to the Constitution, Americans are generally divided into three camps: those who are for it, those who are against it and those who have read it. After reading the next four chapters, I suspect that you will be a member of all three camps.

First, we will discuss the workings of the federal government and its system of checks and balances. Second, we will discuss the relationship between the federal government and the various state and local governments. Lastly, we will explore some of the first ten amendments to the Constitution, the Bill of Rights. Other portions of the Bill of Rights are covered in the criminal law section of this book.

Chapter 16

THE FEDERAL GOVERNMENT
"The Three-Ringed Circus"

The federal government is composed of three branches:

(1) Executive (the President);

(2) Legislative (the Congress); and

(3) Judicial (the courts).

As you may remember from school, the Constitution creates a system of checks and balances. However, currently the government seems to be writing many more checks than it can balance. Nevertheless, this chapter will describe the functions of each branch of government.

THE PRESIDENT

Although the President is often referred to as "The Leader of the Free World," his powers are actually quite limited. The President's primary power is to execute, or carry out, the nation's laws.

Obviously, the President can't carry out the laws by himself, or even, with a handful of highly "motivated" interns. Therefore, the President has the power to appoint his friends, business partners and large campaign contributors to high-ranking cabinet positions to help him in this effort.

The President also plays a *very* limited role in lawmaking. Although not required by the Constitution, Congress allows the President to submit an annual budget for consideration. Often, Congress uses this budget as a starting point in developing the federal budget.

Vetoes

Moreover, the President has veto powers. Each bill passed by Congress is sent to the President for his signature. The President has 10 days to take action on the bill. During this period, he can choose one of three responses.

First, the President can sign the bill, making it a law.

Second, the President

can return the bill to Congress unsigned, thereby *vetoing* it. In this case, Congress can override the veto only with a two-thirds majority vote in *both* houses. In this age of partisan politics, a Congressional override is unlikely. After all, about the only thing that two-thirds of Congress can agree upon is a longer congressional happy hour.

Finally, as a third option, the President can literally do nothing, much like Reagan during his entire second term. If the President neither signs nor vetoes the bill within 10 days,

then it automatically becomes law. Presidents choose this option when they oppose a bill but fear that their veto will be overridden.

However, in some cases, doing nothing can actually defeat the bill. For instance, if the congressional session expires during the 10-day waiting period, then the bill does <u>not</u> become a law but rather expires. In this event, it must be reintroduced in the next session. Therefore, in this case, the President can literally "pocket" the bill, much like a campaign contribution. For obvious reasons, this is called a "pocket veto."

Pardons

The President also has the power to pardon people convicted of federal crimes. In some cases, a pardon completely exonerates the convicted person. In other cases, the pardon simply reduces the sentence.

However, the President doesn't have the power to pardon those convicted in state courts. As a hypothetical example, let's suppose Drug Dealing Danny is currently serving a life sentence in state prison. In this case, Danny can't receive a presidential pardon, even if he hires the President's brother, brother-in-law and his wife's former law partner to lobby on his behalf. About the only thing any of these people can do for Danny is to get him a set of presidential china "mistakenly" taken from the White House during the last days of the administration.

NOTE FROM THE PUBLISHER: This last example was hypothetical and any resemblance to past Presidents serving from 1992 to 2000 is purely coincidental.

Executive Privilege

A commonly misunderstood perk of the presidency is "executive privilege." The President can claim executive privilege to shield military and diplomatic affairs (but not extramarital affairs). However, this privilege is only recognized if the "privileged" information consists of sensitive top-secret information, such as military secrets, the location of strategic forces or the First Lady's dress size.

Foreign Affairs

Finally, the President has a great deal of power over foreign affairs. As commander-in-chief of the armed forces, the President can order military strikes and deploy troops. However, the President can't engage in a lengthy military campaign without Congress' consent or without Hollywood making dozens of movies about it.

As part of his duties as commander-in-chief, the President may make treaties with foreign countries. But once again, this power is checked by the Congress. All treaties must be ratified by the Senate. For instance, let's suppose the President signs a treaty with Canada, trading the state of Maine for a six-pack of Molson Light. Despite the President's action, Maine won't become a part of Canada until the Senate ratifies the treaty, which is highly unlikely unless Canada offers at least a keg.

THE CONGRESS

The Congress is split into two houses: the Senate and the House of Representatives. The Senate is made up of 100 members; two from each state. Each Senator serves a six-year term. These terms are staggered, much like the Senators themselves. As a result, each year, one-third of the Senators are up for re-election.

In contrast, the House of Representatives consists of 435 members, each serving a term of two years. Every two years, the entire membership of the House is up for re-election. Moreover, the number of representatives is not evenly divided among the states but is rather determined by population. Therefore, a very populous state like California has 53 representatives while Idaho, Wyoming and Montana all share the same person. Actually, each state has at least one representative.

The Constitution grants Congress many powers. For instance, Congress has power over interstate commerce, taxing, spending, immigration and war. Moreover, Congress controls the Post Office, the Copyright Office, the Patent Office and the Trademark Office. Also, Congress has the power to fix weights, measures and prize fights. Of course, Congress has delegated this last power to Don King.

And my favorite congressional power is the power to make all laws "necessary and proper" to carry out its other specified powers. As a result of this clause, the power of the federal government is more unchecked than that box on the tax form that asks whether you wish to voluntarily donate $3 to the federal election fund.

THE COURTS

The federal judiciary is composed of three levels:

(1) The district courts;

(2) The appellate courts;

(3) The Supreme Court.

Most cases are originally brought in the district courts. If the losing party wishes to appeal, then she can appeal to the appellate court for that district. The Supreme Court is the final level of appeal from any de-

---

Activities That *Should* Be Taxed by Congress

1. Carrying around a beeper or cell phone if you don't have a job

2. Putting fancy wheels and other accessories on a car with a book value of $300

3. Installing cable television on a black and white TV set

4. Making any of the following films: Rocky VI, Rambo IV or any film starring Pauly Shore

5. Making your 4-year-old child say that he is only 3 years old so he can get into the movies free

cision in the appellate courts.

The Constitution restricts the actions of the federal courts to "cases and controversies." To ensure only actual "cases and controversies" are decided, the Supreme Court has developed standards that must be met to bring a case in federal court.

Standing

One standard is that the plaintiff must have *standing* to bring the case. To have standing, the plaintiff must have a claim of direct injury to him. For instance, let's suppose a city passes an ordinance prohibiting black men from driving cars in nice neighborhoods at night, much like the current "unofficial" policy in many cities. Offenders un-

der this ordinance are given a citation for "DWB" (driving while black) and subjected to extensive questioning and lengthy delays. Obviously, this ordinance is unconstitutional. However, a federal court will not intervene and strike down the ordinance until someone brings a case challenging it.

Furthermore, not just anyone can bring the case. Only black men of driving age can challenge the law. For instance, Jerry Seinfeld can't sue over this ordinance since he won't be harmed by it. This is true even if his chauffeur is black.

Interestingly enough, even Stevie Wonder can't sue under this ordinance as he is not in any danger of being pulled over for DWB. Actually, if he is caught

driving a car in *any* neighborhood, he deserves to be hit with both a citation *and* a nightstick.

Ripeness

Another requirement for "cases and controversies" is that they be "ripe" for a decision. For instance, let's suppose the DWB ordinance has not yet been passed. In this case, a court won't hear a case challenging the ordinance because the case isn't yet "ripe" for hearing by the court.

Mootness

The same is true when the case is "overripe" or moot. For instance, let's suppose Caucasian Carl files a "reverse discrimination" lawsuit against a state university for being denied admission to its law school. Let's further assume that by the time the case reaches the Supreme Court, Carl has already graduated from another law school. In this case, the Supreme Court will likely decide that the issue of reverse discrimination is moot for Carl and refuse to hear his case.

However, there are some situations in which the federal courts will hear moot cases. For example, a person convicted of a crime can challenge his conviction even if he has already served his sentence. This is because the effects of being convicted of a crime – damage to reputation, probation, love letters from former cellmates, etc. – continue even after prison.

In fact, one of the most famous Supreme Court cases in modern history involved a moot issue. By the time *Roe v. Wade* reached the Supreme Court, Baby Roe was already born and obviously, abortion was no longer an option. However, the Supreme Court decided to hear the case anyway because otherwise no woman could ever challenge an abortion law. After all, no case ever reaches the Supreme Court in less than 9 months. In fact, it usually takes longer than 9 months for some of the older justices to climb down from the bench.

A *Lawp*sided View
Weights and Measures

Although the Founding Fathers were able to shake off the rule of the British monarchy, they weren't able to shake off the British (or standard) measurement system. This is not withstanding the fact that the British have long since dumped this ridiculously arcane system. Here's why:

The Stone – This is a unit of weight equal to 14 pounds. Only a person with a single-digit IQ, or member of the British royal family, would base a standard of measure on the number 14? When was the last time you said to someone, "Hey Joe! We're 1/14th the way there!"?

The Mile – A mile is 5,280 feet. Now, I understand that counting out single feet can become cumbersome but it would have never occurred to me (or any person whose brain receives a constant supply of oxygen) to group these individual feet into units of 5,280.

The Acre – After searching the web for six straight days, I discovered that an acre is equal to 43,560 sq. ft. How is a child supposed to remember that?

Is it any wonder our kids perform so miserably in school? After spending a day trying to remember the number of quarts in a gallon, the number of yards in a hectare and the number of automatic weapons in their lockers, they are exhausted!

Chapter in Review
The Federal Government

1. **The three branches of government are:**
   a. Fig, oak and palm
   b. Crooked, more crooked and tangled
   c. Executive, legislative and judicial

2. **Who is primarily responsible for foreign affairs?**
   a. The President
   b. Congress
   c. Julio Iglesias

3. **Which of the following powers has NOT been granted to Congress?**
   a. The power to tax and spend
   b. The power to NOT tax and spend so much
   c. The power to declare war

Chapter 17

FEDERALISM
Those Pesky Little States

This chapter discusses the interaction between the federal government and the various state governments. As drafted, the Constitution grants *limited* powers to the federal government. All other powers are granted to the states.

Therefore, *in theory*, the states have exclusive control over law enforcement, education, health and welfare issues, etc. However, *in reality*, nothing could be further from the truth, except, of course, for Robert Blake's "I left my gun in the restaurant" alibi. The truth of the matter is that, over time, the federal government has found ways to expand its influence into virtually every area of state control.

The Brady Bill is a good example of the federal government's intrusion into traditionally state-controlled areas. The Brady Bill was a gun control law that imposed a *nationwide* five-day waiting period for handgun purchases.

This federal scheme of gun control is not what the Founding Fathers had in mind when they designed the Constitution. They envisioned a country in which each state would decide its own gun control scheme, if any. Under this patchwork system of state laws, Michigan would have a five-day waiting period, while Washington would have a five-*year* waiting period and, in Oklahoma, guns would be available in vending machines. However,

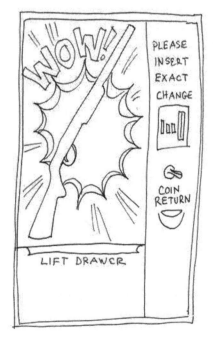

despite the Founding Fathers' intentions, the federal government's power has expanded almost as rapidly as my waistline.

In doing so, the federal government has relied on other constitutional principles, including:

- **Preemption**

- **Interstate Commerce**

- **Taxing and Spending**

- **Privileges and Immunities**

PREEMPTION

The Supremacy Clause of the Constitution makes the federal law the supreme law of the land. As a result, any state law that *directly conflicts* with a federal law will be overruled, or *preempted*. For instance, let's suppose the federal government outlaws the possession of guns by anyone *under* the age of 65. This new federal law would conflict with a long-standing Texas law that requires all persons over the age of 12 to carry at least one gun at all times (even in the shower). As a result of the Supremacy Clause, the Texas law would be preempted.

In some cases, it isn't so easy to determine whether the state law directly conflicts with the federal law. For instance, let's suppose a federal law requires all children less than 4 years of age to sit in a child safety seat while riding in a car. Furthermore, let's suppose the State of Washington decides to go one step further and apply the car seat law to all passengers riding in a car.

Of course, unless manufacturers begin making those seats *much* bigger, someone will challenge this law. Nevertheless, this state law might withstand challenge because it doesn't *directly* conflict with federal safety regulations, but rather just adds to them.

However, in some cases, a state law will be overturned even if it doesn't directly conflict with a federal law. This is the case where the federal government has its own regulatory scheme and the state law would upset it.

For instance, let's suppose the federal government finally decides to tackle a serious problem in America – flavored coffees. In the past, it was possible to walk into a coffee shop and order a cup of coffee in less than an hour. But now, it takes that long just to go through all of the caffeine choices – caffeinated, decaffeinated, diet decaffeinated, clear, etc.

After studying the problem for 15 years at a cost of more than $600 million, the FCC, Flavored Coffee Commission, sets national standards for coffee ordering. Under this new system, a customer must only ask for a #53 to purchase a "Medium Decaf Mocca Latte Espresso Foamed Cinnamon Edged Chocolate Sprinkled with Raspberry Torte Cream and 1 1/4 packets of Brown Sugar."

Even with this great improvement, Tennessee goes one step further and directly outlaws the sale of all "sissy coffees" in the state. In this case, the Tennessee law would be preempted because the federal government looked into the problem and, after careful consideration, chose not to outlaw sissy coffees. To allow any state to outlaw particular coffees might ruin the numbering scheme that cost the American people in excess of $600 million, which is the cost of one B-1 bomber, two gold-plated toilet seats or three #68s.

INTERSTATE COMMERCE

The Constitution expressly forbids the states from interfering with interstate commerce. Therefore, if a state law burdens interstate commerce, it will be overturned faster than a police cruiser after the Los Angeles Lakers win an NBA championship.

As a result, a state law that discriminates against citizens from other states is unconstitutional. For instance, a state tax of $100 on every carton of milk produced out-of-state would be unconstitutional. Also, a state law forbidding the importation of out-of-state milk would be unconstitutional.

However, there is one situation in which a state can discriminate against citizens of another state. This is when the state provides the product or service itself. Therefore, a state-owned dairy may sell milk only to its own citizens. In fact, if so inclined, it could instruct its delivery drivers to drive along the borders of neighboring states taunting "foreign" children with false promises of chocolate milk and ice cream.

Of course, few state legislatures are brazen enough to enact clearly discriminatory laws. Nevertheless, even "neutral" laws will be struck down if they *unduly burden* interstate commerce.

For instance, let's suppose a state passes a law outlawing the display of "plumber's crack." Obviously, this ordinance will apply to citizens and non-citizens alike. However, this law could unduly burden interstate commerce because the primary offenders would be long-distance truck drivers sitting at the counter at Denny's. Since it seems impossible for truck drivers to either wear pants that fit properly or avoid a good special at Denny's, a court might decide that the law unduly burdens interstate commerce.

In fact, the Supreme Court used the interstate commerce clause to invalidate segregation laws during the 1960s. The court struck down state laws preventing African-Americans from being served in restaurants and hotels by declaring that these laws unduly burdened interstate commerce.

TAXING AND SPENDING

The Constitution states that "Congress shall have power to lay and collect taxes, duties, imposts and excises...." As you know, this is a power that Congress seldom fails to use.

Before the 20th century, the federal government only used excise and sales taxes to raise revenue. However, in the late 1800s, the federal government introduced an income tax. In 1895, the Supreme Court ruled that Congress did <u>not</u> have the power to levy income taxes.

Incredibly, it was the American people, themselves, who granted Congress the power to levy income taxes under the 16th Amendment. Not surprisingly, just six years later, the Constitution was once again amended to ban the sale of intoxicating liquors.

The federal government uses its taxing power for a number of purposes. Obviously, it uses taxes to raise revenue. It also uses taxes to encourage certain activities and discourage others. For instance, the federal government allows homeowners to deduct home mortgage interest while no such deduction is available to renters. As a result, citizens are *encouraged* to buy homes rather than rent them.

Likewise, the government imposes taxes on alcohol and tobacco in an effort to discourage consumption of these substances. These are so-called "sin taxes." Unfortunately, Congress does not tax other sins, such as gluttony, lust or greed. This is unfortunate because the revenue generated from athletes, entertainers and Enron executives alone would be enough to balance the federal budget.

The federal government also regulates activities through its spending power. Much like my wife, the federal government spends money on a dizzying number of things. For instance, the federal government provides billions of dollars of state and local aid for education, highway projects and other purposes.

However, in many cases, this assistance comes with more strings attached than a "free" weekend at a timeshare resort. For instance, the federal government has required states to increase their minimum drinking

ages from 18 to 21 in order to receive certain highway grants.

PRIVILEGES AND IMMUNITIES

The Constitution states, "The Citizens of each State shall be entitled to all of the Privileges and Immunities of Citizens in the several States." In English, this means that a state can't deny basic rights to citizens of another state. These basic rights are the rights to earn a living, travel freely between the states and access the court system.

For instance, let's suppose the people of a wealthy state, Richland, would like to prevent the people of a neighboring state, Poorland, from coming into Richland for employment opportunities, cultural events and indoor plumbing. As a result, Richland's government passes a law requiring proof of Richland citizenship to work in the state. As a result of the privileges and immunities clause, this law would be struck down immediately.

In some cases, states attempt to get around this clause by passing seemingly "neutral" laws that, in actuality, are not neutral at all. For instance, let's suppose the state of Countryland requires all persons to know the words to Billy Ray Cyrus' *Achy Breaky Heart* in order to enter into the state. As a result of this law, few people from the state of Rapland are able to make it past the border checkpoint. In this case, Countryland's law would be struck down unless it could demonstrate that the law is related to some *substantial* state interest.

INDIVIDUAL LIBERTIES

The remaining chapters in this section involve individual freedoms guaranteed by the Constitution. Some of these freedoms are guaranteed in the body of the Constitution and others are covered in the first 10 Amendments to the Constitution, the Bill of Rights.

One very important thing to remember about these constitutional freedoms is that they only protect you from actions by federal, state and local agencies. These freedoms do not protect you from the actions of private citizens.

As a child, I learned this lesson the hard way. After learning about the First Amendment in school, I attempted to assert my right to free speech in the face of my father's command to "Shut up!" I quickly (and painfully) learned that fathers need not grant freedom of speech to their children. As a married man, I'm slowly learning that this same principle applies to my wife as well.

Finally, the Constitution only protects you from interference with the exercise of your rights. It doesn't require government to provide you with the means to exercise your rights. For instance, Lazy Leonard has a basic right to make a living. However, the government doesn't have to provide him with a job. Although with a name like Lazy Leonard, he seems perfectly suited for a job at the Department of Motor Vehicles.

Chapter in Review
Federalism

1. The Supremacy Clause states that:
    a. Federal law is the supreme law of the land
    b. Momma's word is law
    c. Diana Ross is the most popular of the Supremes

2. Excise taxes on alcohol and tobacco are called:
    a. Bull#$%^!
    b. Sin taxes
    c. All of the above

3. Which of the following is NOT considered a "basic right?"
    a. The right to work
    b. The right to travel freely amongst the states
    c. Making a right on red

Chapter 18

THE FIRST AMENDMENT
The Freedom to Pray, Bitch and Moan

History books often suggest that the Founding Fathers started the American Revolution in order to secure the rights of free speech, religion and a free press. Although the truth is probably less glamorous (e.g., they were trying to get away from that terrible British food), our First Amendment freedoms are among the most cherished.

The First Amendment to the Constitution states, "Congress shall make no law respecting an *establishment of religion*, or prohibiting the *free exercise* thereof, abridging the *freedom of speech*, or of *the press*, or the right of the people peaceably to *assemble*, and to petition the Government for a redress of grievances."

FREEDOM OF RELIGION

There are two basic parts to the freedom of religion:

(1) the government shall not *establish* religion;

(2) the government shall not restrict anyone's belief in religion.

As always in the law, these rules are subject to various exceptions and qualifications.

Establishment of Religion

The Establishment Clause prevents the United States from establishing a national religion. It also prevents the government from establishing religious schools.

Moreover, the government can't do much to aid students attending private religious schools. In one landmark case, the court ruled that it was unconstitutional to provide tax breaks and reimbursement of transportation costs for students attending private religious schools.

Furthermore, the government can do almost nothing to support religion in *public* schools. For instance, the courts have repeatedly ruled that schools can't set aside time for prayer, even non-denominational, silent prayer. However, despite these rulings, so long as there are pop quizzes, weekly hostage situations and cafeteria food, prayer will remain a vital part of the public school system.

Dear God...

Free Exercise of Religion

On the other hand, the government can't infringe upon a person's religious beliefs. For instance, the government may not mandate or outlaw the belief in a particular religion.

Furthermore, the government can't make benefits contingent upon belonging to a certain religion. Therefore, it can't require a person to profess a belief in God in order to receive handouts of government cheese. To do so would be unconstitutional and silly because trust me, after eating government cheese, *everyone* starts praying to God.

However, it becomes more complicated when a person's religious actions violate a law that doesn't have a religious basis. In this situation, a court will balance the individual's right to exercise his religion against the state's interest in preventing harm. For instance, let's suppose Bigamist Ben's religious beliefs *require* him to marry more than one woman at a time. In this case, Ben's religious beliefs will be outweighed by the state's interests in ensuring the sanctity of both marriage and joint filing status on Form 1040.

In other cases, a court will decide that a person's freedom of religion outweighs the government's interest in enforcing the law.

When Freedom of Religion is Too Much

Although freedom of religion is a fundamental and cherished freedom in our country, the following "religious" practices should be outlawed:

- A professional boxer thanking God for giving him the strength to knock his opponent unconscious.

- A musician thanking God for giving him the inspiration to write the triple platinum hit, "I Want to [Bleep] [Bleep] [Bleep] All Night!"

- People who go to church on Easter Sunday when they haven't gone to church on any of the other 51 Sundays in the year.

For instance, let's suppose Paranoid Paul believes that sleeping on a mattress with a federally mandated tag will send him "straight to Hell." In this case, Paul may remove the tag without going to prison because the government's interest in having all mattresses properly tagged is not compelling enough to justify sending Paul "straight to Hell." However, the government would be justified in sending Paul "straight to a *psychiatrist.*"

FREEDOM OF SPEECH

It is important to clarify that when the term "speech" is used in this chapter, it refers to writings, pictures and other forms of expression, as well as spoken words.

The government may attempt to restrict speech by either regulating:

- **The content of the speech; or**

- **The time, place and manner of the speech.**

Content

When the government regulation is based on the *content* of the speech, then the government has the burden of proving that the restriction is *absolutely necessary* or that the speech is "unprotected" speech. Incredibly enough, the courts have actually determined that some speech is unworthy of constitutional protection. These categories of "unprotected speech" are unfortunately some of my favorite kinds:

- **Communications likely to incite violence** ("Let's get him!");

- **Obscenity** (definitely one of my favorites);

- **Defamation** (easily two-thirds of the jokes in this book); and

- **Commercial speech** ("You too can become a millionaire if you come to my *free* seminar!").

However, if the speech is a *protected* form of speech, then the government can restrict it only for compelling reasons, such as national security. Therefore, the government can prevent someone from publishing military secrets, strategic alliances or the ingredients of the special sauce on the Big Mac.

In other cases, it is unclear whether the government has a compelling enough reason to restrict speech. For instance, let's suppose a certain witty, insightful and sexy legal humorist travels the country educating the public about the law. Not surprisingly, this tour results in thousands of women leaving their husbands now that they've seen a "real man."

A *Lawpsided* View
Obscenity

Although everyone seems to agree that the Constitution doesn't protect obscene speech, almost no one can seem to agree upon what is "obscene." Nevertheless, over the years, the Supreme Court has developed the following definition. Speech is obscene if:

1. The average person, applying contemporary community standards, would find that the speech excites lustful thoughts;

2. The speech shows sexual conduct in a patently offensive way; and

3. The speech lacks serious literary, artistic, political, or scientific value.

Unfortunately, this "definition" is both unclear and disturbing for a number of reasons.

For one, the definition of obscenity changes depending upon the geographical location. Therefore, in some parts of the country, Pampers ads showing little baby butts would be obscene. On the other hand, in a place like Las Vegas, nothing would be obscene (which is why I'm moving there as soon as I can sell enough copies of this book).

Although I am not a constitutional scholar (or even fully literate, for that matter), this seems wrong. After all, shouldn't federal constitutional rights be applicable in all states? Surely, no one would suggest we allow communities to determine for themselves whether their citizens may vote, work or marry their third cousins.

Secondly, the legal status of speech shouldn't be determined by whether it excites lustful thoughts. After all, almost everything excites lustful thoughts in men. For instance, I have witnessed grown men debate for hours over whom is sexier – Wilma Flintstone or Betty Rubble? In one instance, the debate turned into a fistfight (for the record, he hit me first). Does this mean that The Flintstones is obscene?

Finally, speech shouldn't lose its protected status merely because its lacks serious literary, artistic, political or scientific *value*. After all, like beauty, value is in the eye of the beholder. For instance, a performance that is trashy, crass, vulgar, violent and just plain silly to one person may be worth $39.95 on pay-per-view to a professional wrestling fan like me.

In this case, the government would have a compelling reason to stop the tour. Nevertheless, my right to free speech would probably *outweigh* the government's interest in securing stable families (at least, until my wife steps onto the "scales of justice" in this matter).

Time, Place and Manner

In the case of time, place and manner regulations, the analysis is slightly different. So long as the regulation is content neutral, then the regulation will likely be upheld as constitutional. A regulation is content neutral if it applies to liberals and conservatives, Democrats and Republicans, and environmentalists and sane people alike.

However, whether a regulation is truly content neutral is sometimes difficult to determine. For instance, let's suppose a town passes an ordinance prohibiting protests after dark. On its face, this ordinance seems content neutral but what about the vampire population?

When could they exercise their constitutional rights?

If this book does anything, I hope that it can shed some light on the persecution suffered daily by the *sunlightedly* challenged.

Also, the place *where* the speech occurs can be significant. For instance, some places are considered traditional public forums, such as parks, city hall and daytime talk shows. Free speech can *never* be banned completely in these places but can be regulated by reasonable rules. Therefore, a city may not ban protests at city hall by the American Association of Retired Persons but it may ban *nude* protests at city hall by AARP.

And there are some government properties, such as military bases, where free speech can be banned altogether, or at least severely limited. Therefore, even if AARP members agree to remain clothed at all times, they won't be allowed to protest *inside* the Pentagon.

In some cases, even private property can be considered a public forum. For instance, some states require private shopping mall owners to allow access to people passing out political pamphlets. Unfortunately, these states don't require mall owners to build adequate parking nearby. Therefore, as a practical matter, by the time protestors find parking spaces, their cause is usually more outdated than my father's wardrobe.

Freedom of the Press

For the most part, the press has the same right to free speech as anyone else. As a result, the press is only free from *governmental* restrictions. On the other hand, individual privacy and property rights will often trump the rights of the press. For instance, the press can't break into Cindy Crawford's home to shoot footage of her in the tub and then claim freedom of the press (damn!).

Other Freedoms Enjoyed by the Press

1. The freedom to run the same story *every* day and still call it "breaking news" (i.e., Zippergate, the death of Princess Di, weather reports in southern California, etc.).

2. The freedom to put 35 commercials in the last two minutes of a sporting event.

3. The freedom to ruin every Sunday evening by showing a sappy "chick movie" that my wife insists I watch with her.

However, the press does have the right to cover the workings of the government and to report on matters of public record. Therefore, if Cindy Crawford is rolled into court in her *bathtub*, we may actually get to see those photos after all.

In some cases, the public's right to information concerning criminal proceedings conflicts with the defendant's right to a fair trial. In these cases, pretrial media coverage can diminish the defendant's chances in court. Nevertheless, freedom of the press usually prevails if the judge can use other means to assure a fair trial for the defendant.

For example, let's suppose the fictional sportscaster, Perv Alpert, is arrested for sexual assault. Obviously, media coverage of the case may reduce Alpert's chance of receiving a fair trial lower than his chances of ever getting another date. Nevertheless, rather than banning media coverage, the judge may choose to change the venue of the trial or sequester the jury.

In some cases, a judge will impose a gag order on the parties and their lawyers to prevent them from speaking with the press. Unfortunately, judges can't prevent *all* lawyers from speaking about the case, just those actually involved. As a result, the TV viewing public will continue to witness the spectacle of 50 "legal commentators" all saying the same thing repeatedly on CNN.

The two media outlets subject to the most governmental control are television and radio. This is because the airwaves are limited and each broadcaster is given a license to use them at the expense of others. As a result, the FCC has the authority to regulate TV and radio broadcasters to make sure that they don't do anything crazy, like broadcast shows that are actually informative and entertaining.

In the past, broadcasters were subjected to the "fairness doctrine." This doctrine required broadcasters to give free airtime to people with opposing political views. In recent years, the fairness doctrine has been abandoned. This is fortunate for cable television stations like *The Lifetime Channel* ("Television for Women Who Hate Men"). Under the fairness doctrine, it would have been required to run *hourly* editorials by Andrew Dice Clay.

FREEDOM OF ASSOCIATION

The freedom of association is the freedom of individuals to join together to exercise rights of free speech, to petition the government, or to worship. Unfortunately, the right to get together for a wild party is not constitutionally protected.

Also, please note that in most cases, the freedom of association is a voluntary right. For example, Lonely Larry can't abduct Charlie's Angels and then claim "freedom of association." To enjoy this freedom, the other people in the group must also want to associate with you.

However, this isn't always the case with large groups. For instance, some states require all-male or all-white clubs to open their doors to women and minority members. This is despite the clubs' claim that this violates their freedom of association.

However, the courts have ruled that "forced integration" is constitutional, so long as the association between the members is not *intimate.* Put simply, the more personal the relationship between the members, the greater their flexibility to *arbitrarily* choose who can become a member.

As a result, each of us is completely free to be restrictive in choosing a mate. Unfortunately, this is not a freedom utilized by many of the women in my family.

Now, assuming you are a member of an association, can you be punished strictly for being a member? The answer is "No." For instance, if you join Amway, you won't be *automatically* prosecuted for taking advantage of your friends and family to unload the $20,000 of product you were duped into buying at the big sales meeting. To be prosecuted, you must first call each of them and tell them about the great "opportunity" that you would like to "share" with them.

One of the most contested issues in this area is whether a group can be forced to disclose its membership list. As a general matter, the group can only be forced to disclose its membership when there is some compelling government interest.

For instance, let's suppose Freaky Freddy is the president of a swinger's organization. One day, he is approached by Bill Clinton's secret service agents, who demand he disclose his membership list. In this case, Freddy doesn't have to comply. Clinton's interest in obtaining dating prospects is not compelling enough to justify violating the organization's rights.

Chapter in Review
The First Amendment

1.   A government-sponsored religious school is unconstitutional because:

   a.   It is an establishment of religion

   b.   It violates free speech

   c.   Guvermint and edumacation just don't micks

2.   Who is sexier – Wilma Flintstone or Betty Rubble?

   a.   Wilma Flintstone

   b.   Betty Rubble

   c.   Neither! They are just cartoon characters. Get a life!

3.   A judge may impose a gag order if:

   a.   He has eaten my wife's cooking

   b.   He has just seen Janet Reno in a teddy

   c.   Media coverage will prevent a fair trial

Chapter 10

OTHER CONSTITUTIONAL FREEDOMS
"I'll Take Potpourri For $200, Alex!"

THE RIGHT TO BEAR ARMS

Although much of the Constitution seems to have been written in a language other than English, the wording of the Second Amendment is relatively clear. It states that "the right of the people to keep and bear arms shall not be infringed."

Moreover, the historical context of its enactment makes the meaning even clearer. During the American Revolution, the colonists faced hardships because the British had outlawed them from having weapons. With this in mind, the framers of the Constitution set out to ensure that the people would have a means to fight back if the newly formed American government ever became arrogant and all-powerful.

In short, the Second Amendment was not enacted to protect the rights of sportsmen, hobbyists or postal employees. The purpose of this amendment was to allow citizens to *revolt*.

Of course, the Founding Fathers lived in a time when weapons had limited destructive power. For instance, a person armed with a musket was only *slightly* more dangerous than a person wielding a club, a slingshot or a fully loaded water pistol.

Unfortunately, over the last 200 years, weapons have become almost as destructive as my two sons. Therefore, courts fear that a literal interpretation of the Second Amendment would allow private citizens to own tanks, attack helicopters and even, nuclear weapons. As a result, courts regularly limit the right to keep and bear arms.

TAKINGS

It has been long established that governments have the power to take private property by *eminent domain*. A common example is when the state takes land to build a highway or a $400 million stadium for a sports franchise that will invariably insist upon another new stadium in two years.

Nevertheless, the Fifth Amendment restricts the eminent domain power. For one, eminent domain may be used only for a *public use*. Second, the government must provide the owner with *just compensation* for the taking.

Interestingly, a government can use eminent domain to take property for its own use or for the use of private citizens or corporations. In either case, it will fulfill the public use requirement so long as the taking accomplishes a *legitimate governmental goal*. And the courts are usually generous in recognizing a legitimate governmental goal.

For instance, let's suppose Raider Ron, a homeowner in Kansas City, paints his house silver and black, the colors of the city's major football rival, the Oakland Raiders. Coincidentally, this very disturbed individual lives next door to the mayor. At the direction of the mayor, the city takes Ron's house by eminent domain, paints it red, white and gold (the colors of the Kansas City Chiefs) and then sells it to a private citizen (one with *extremely* bad taste).

If challenged in court, the city will lose if Ron can show that his house was taken to please the mayor since that wouldn't be for a public purpose. On the other hand, if the city can demonstrate that it took the property to prevent riots in the streets between deranged fans of the Raiders and Chiefs, it will prevail. Nevertheless, even if the city successfully withstands Ron's challenge, it will be required to compensate Ron for the value of his home.

However, in some situations, it is unclear whether the government's action is a "taking" and therefore, requires just compensation. In some cases, instead of taking actual ownership of the property, the government simply passes regulations restricting its use.

As a general rule, these regulations are not considered "takings." As a result, governments can pass laws regulating certain behavior without providing just compensation. For instance, let's suppose Don Juan Domingo Ricardo Carlos Venezuela uses a warehouse in the town of Hip-

pyopia to distribute cocaine. True to its name, the town of Hippyopia has no drug laws.

Let's further suppose that the residents of this town sober up one day and ban the distribution of narcotics.

As a result, the value of Venezuela's warehouse plummets almost as fast as the value of any stock immediately after I buy it. Nevertheless, Venezuela can't sue the town by claiming that the law is a "taking" of his property. Nor can he request to be compensated for his lost profits of $7 million per day.

However, there are some regulations that are takings, such as those that grant other people rights to the property. For instance, let's suppose the town of Liberalurbia decides to fight

Takings That Are Not Compensated

1. When your mother made you share your Halloween candy with your little sister.

2. When your spouse takes up most of the bed and steals all the covers (in addition to the last of your hopes and dreams of happiness).

homelessness by requiring all homeowners to open their doors to the homeless at night. In this case, the town will have to reimburse the homeowners for the costs of fumigating their homes on a daily basis and replacing liquor that "mysteriously" disappears during the night.

NOTE FROM THE PUBLISHER: Lawpsided Press would like to apologize for these gross generalizations about the homeless. In fact, we invite all readers who are currently homeless to sleep at our office during the evening. We are located at 1600 Pennsylvania Avenue, Washington, D.C.

DUE PROCESS

The Fifth Amendment also guarantees that no person will be deprived of life, liberty, or property without *due process of law.* Due process of law is required in criminal trials where the state is attempting to take away the defendant's liberty or perhaps, his life. Due process is also required when the govern-

ment attempts to deprive citizens of other liberty interests, such as the right to earn a living or maintain certain family relationships.

Also, certain property interests are protected by the due process requirement, such as licenses. Therefore, in order for the government to take away your license to drive a car, it must comply with due process (or just keep raising the insurance requirement until you can no longer afford both a car *and* insurance).

One of the most interesting property interests protected by the due process requirement is the "right" to receive welfare benefits. Welfare recipients are *entitled* to welfare and must continue receiving it until terminated by due process of law, or by marriage to a second cousin.

Of course, this begs the question: what are the requirements of due process? In criminal cases, these procedures can be quite complex – pre-trial hearing, bail hearing, low-speed chase in a Ford Bronco, etc. In civil cases, the procedures don't have to be so

formal.

However, due process *always* requires prior notice of the governmental action. Also, due process usually requires a hearing to allow the person to protest the action. Often the issue in due process cases is whether this hearing must be held before or after the government takes away the right.

The answer largely depends upon the importance of the right being taken away. For instance, a hearing is required *before* welfare benefits can be terminated. This is because welfare benefits are often the person's only means of support.

In the last 50 years, courts have pushed the concept of due process past mere procedural requirements. The courts have ruled that *fundamental due process* requires recognition of a right to privacy. As a result, the government may not regulate activities covered by this right of privacy *at all*.

The right to privacy is most often associated with a woman's right to choose abortion. It is important to note that this right is strictly a woman's right. Therefore, the biological father has no right to either compel or veto the woman's decision about an abortion.

In the case of a minor, the government may require parental notification before an abortion. However, it must set up a procedure where a judge can dispense with parental notification if he determines that the minor is mature enough to make her own decision.

Lastly, although a woman has a fundamental right to privacy with respect to abortion, her right is not unlimited. After the first three months of the pregnancy, the government may take reasonable precautions to protect the lives of the mother and the fetus. And at some point in the pregnancy, the government may prohibit an abortion altogether.

Of course, there are other rights of privacy as well, such as the right to contraceptives, the right to refuse medical care and the right of related persons to live together. Therefore, my neighbors have a constitutionally protected right to

cram 17 adults, 13 kids *and* 6 dogs into the tiny 3-bedroom house next door.

However, their constitutional right to lower my property value doesn't prevent me from giving them dirty looks and talking about them behind their backs. After all, I have constitutional rights too.

Despite the numerous rights of privacy, the courts have refused to grant unlimited rights to privacy, particularly in the area of sex (damn courts!). However, as a general rule, the courts frown upon restrictions affecting sexual relations between married persons, particularly if they happen to be married to *each other*. On the other hand, the courts will allow restrictions affecting sexual relations between unmarried couples, particularly those of the same sex.

EQUAL PROTECTION

The 14th Amendment states, "no state shall ... deny to any person ... the *equal protection* of the laws." The purpose of this amendment is to prevent the government from discriminating against certain groups. However, as you will see, discrimination against some groups is more "constitutional" than discrimination against others.

Depending upon the group involved, discrimination is judged under three separate bases:

(1) The Strict Scrutiny Standard

(2) The Rational Basis Standard

(3) The Intermediate Scrutiny Standard

Strict Scrutiny

Governmental discrimination on the basis of race or national origin is the most suspect form of discrimination and is judged under the *strict scrutiny* standard. Under this standard, a law that discriminates against citizens on the basis of race will be struck down unless the government can prove that it is absolutely necessary to further a compelling governmental interest.

As a general rule, laws judged under this standard are almost always struck down. The only exception is for affirmative action programs that are challenged by whites.

However, even affirmative action has its constitutional limits. Affirmative action is only permitted when it is narrowly tailored to meet specific past discrimination.

For instance, let's take the following purely hypothetical example. Let's suppose that there was a group of people who were in America long before the Pilgrims ever set foot on Plymouth Rock. Let's further suppose that these people were driven from their lands and forced to live on reservations in areas where the land was less fertile than Bob Dole. Now, I know such a thing could have never happened in America but just humor me for the sake of this example.

Let's further suppose that, decades later, states attempted to remedy this past discrimination by pro-viding these groups with casino monopolies. In this purely *hypothetical* example, the courts would allow this type of affirmative action, so long as the judges are given free ringside tickets to boxing matches.

The Rational Basis Standard

Finally, although strict scrutiny is usually applied in cases of racial discrimi-

nation, it isn't applied in cases where there is no discriminatory intent. This is the case even if the law results in a *disparate impact* upon members of different races.

For instance, in some cases, the tests used by police departments, fire departments and *Who Wants to be a Millionaire?* result in few minority candidates being selected. Nevertheless, the use of these tests is not judged under the strict scrutiny standard but rather under a much less stringent standard, the *rational basis* standard.

Under this standard, if the law or regulation has a rational relation to *any* conceivable legitimate legislative purpose, then it will be upheld. Obviously, this standard is easier to meet than an aspiring actress (a.k.a. waitress) in southern California.

In age discrimination cases, courts have applied this lowest standard of scrutiny. This is somewhat surprising considering that the average age of the justices on the Supreme Court is *deceased*.

Nevertheless, the high court has repeatedly refused to grant the elderly any special constitutional protection from discrimination. Therefore, so long as the law is *at all* reasonable, it will be found to be constitutional.

Intermediate Scrutiny

Discrimination on the basis of gender is judged under the *intermediate scrutiny* standard. Under this standard, laws that discriminate between the sexes will be upheld so long as they are *substantially related* to an *important governmental interest*.

For instance, let's suppose Ru Paul is elected Mayor of Cincinnati. (If this seems too farfetched for you, keep in mind that Jerry Springer was once mayor of this city.) At Mayor Paul's urging, the city passes an ordinance restricting women from wearing skirts but allowing men to continue doing so. If this ordinance is challenged, its constitutionality will depend upon its purpose.

If the purpose of the law is to ensure that Ru Paul is the best dressed "woman" in town, then the law will be overturned because it isn't substantially related to an important governmental interest.   On the other hand, if the law's purpose is to protect the eyesight of the men of Cincinnati, then the law is constitutional.

Please note that these various standards of review only apply to the courts' analysis of equal protection claims. As you may know, federal and state govern- ments have passed numer- ous laws outlawing dis- crimination in employment and housing, just to name a few. Many of these laws set forth their own stan- dards for judging whether a law or practice is valid. As a result, under many of these laws, victims of gen- der and age discrimination are entitled to the same level of protection as vic- tims of racial discrimina- tion (i.e., not much).

Chapter in Review
Other Constitutional Freedoms

1. The right to bear arms is often relied upon by:

    a.   Professional wrestlers

    b.   The National Rifle Association

    c.   Madonna

2. Under the 5th Amendment, a governmental "taking" requires:

    a.   Just compensation

    b.   A fast getaway car

    c.   Courage

3. Under the due process requirement, a prior hearing is required when:

    a.   The plaintiff has a really good lawyer

    b.   The interest at stake is trivial

    c.   The interest at stake is important

CRIMINAL LAW

IF IT DOES NOT FIT, MUST YOU ACQUIT?

CRIMINAL LAW
OVERVIEW

According to recent statistics, 5.7 million Americans are either in prison, on parole or on probation. And this number is growing daily. In fact, given current growth rates, by the year 2043, the number of Americans in prison will surpass the total number of Americans. Therefore, please pay careful attention to the material in this section of the book so that you don't add to these numbers.

In this section, we will discuss the basic elements of a crime. We will also discuss certain crimes in detail. Of course, it isn't possible to cover all the crimes on the books. Therefore, in these three chapters, we only deal with the major crimes – murder, arson, eating meat on Holy Friday, etc. Lastly, we will discuss the various loopholes available to you in the event you ever find yourself on the wrong side of the law.

Of course, it is my hope (and expectation) that you never encounter any of these principles in your own life. Moreover, even if you do, I implore you to obtain competent legal representation. Remember, the life sentence you serve could be your own.

Nevertheless, the knowledge in this section can be helpful in following breaking news stories, criminal trials or even your favorite sports team. After all, in today's society, the most compelling sports drama occurs *in* the courts not on the courts.

Chapter 20

ELEMENTS OF A CRIME
All That Is Latin

A crime usually requires two things:

(1) a physical act, or *actus reus*; and

(2) a particular mental state, or *mens rea*.

In order to commit a crime, an offender must commit a physical act *while* in the appropriate mental state.

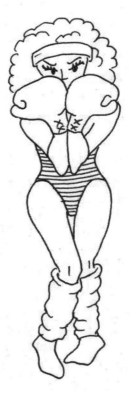

For example, let's suppose Jane Fonda and Media Darling team up to produce a workout video. During the taping, Jane accidentally punches Ms. Darling while performing an aerobics routine. After the release of the video, reviewers note that Ms. Darling is younger, prettier and more talented than Jane. Jane is now glad she accidentally hit Darling and would like to do so again (this time *much* harder).

In this case, Jane Fonda is not guilty of a crime because she did not perform the *actus reus* (hitting Media Darling) at the same time she had the required *mens rea* (wanting to hit her). On the other hand, the fact that she continually sells workout videos to the same group of people who did not get results from the previous videos should be a crime.

ACTUS REUS

To commit a crime, a person must commit a *physical* act. Merely wishing that the guy who stole your girlfriend would die is not a crime. However, wishing he would die while swinging an ax at his head is a crime. Unless, of course, either of you is from New Jersey.

Likewise, the act must be *voluntary*. For instance, let's suppose Epileptic Ernie is riding on a crowded bus. Unexpectedly, Ernie has a severe seizure, which causes him to accidentally injure the little old lady sitting next to him. In this case, Ernie is not guilty of a crime, even if the injured little old lady is his mother-in-law (and she had it coming to her).

Lastly, the offender must not only commit a voluntary physical act but the act must actually *cause* harm to the victim. For instance, sticking a pin through the heart of a voodoo doll of your hated rival is <u>not</u> murder. This is true even if she happens to die from an immediate heart attack. Nevertheless, you should probably get rid of the voodoo doll ... *just in case.*

In some cases, a person can commit a crime by not acting. However, this is only when the person has a legal duty to act. For instance, fathers have a legal duty to care for their children, except during *Monday Night Football.*

However, in general, there are no "Good Samaritan" laws requiring people to come to the aid of complete strangers, or even close friends. This explains why a married man's friends can lawfully encourage him to stay out late when they know that the likely consequence will be a frying pan to the head.

MENS REA

A basic principle of criminal law is that a person is not guilty of a crime unless he commits some harmful action with a criminal intent (the *mens rea*). Each crime requires a particular mental state.

Specific Intent

For some crimes, like attempted murder, the offender must have a *specific intent* to commit the crime. The fact that the offender was "up to no good" is not enough. The offender must have *specifically intended* to cause the harm.

For example, let's suppose Prankster Patty is invited to her grandmother's house for Sunday dinner with Reverend Give-til-it-Hurts. While Grandma is not looking, Patty places a whoopee cushion on her chair. Grandma sits in the chair and the cushion makes the intended sound. Grandma, who is not always in *complete* control of her bodily functions, assumes that she has passed gas in front of the Reverend. At this point, Grandma nearly drops dead from embarrassment.

While Patty's actions in this case were immature and childish (and a little bit funny), she is not guilty of attempted murder. This is because Patty did not have the *specific intent* to kill her grandmother.

Malice

Other crimes, such as murder and arson, require a less specific intent – malice. Malice is *reckless disregard* to the danger caused by one's actions.

For example, shooting an Uzi into a crowd at the Post Office demonstrates reckless disregard for the safety of others and thus, is malicious. If someone is killed in the shooting, the offender is guilty of murder.

Recklessness and Negligence

Crimes like involuntary manslaughter require a lesser form of intent. For these crimes, if the offender

is reckless or negligent, then he may be charged with a crime.

Strict Liability

Lastly, there are a few crimes that do not require any *mens rea*. These are called "strict liability" offenses. For these crimes, if you commit the unlawful act, then you are guilty, regardless of your state of mind.

One example is the crime of selling liquor to a minor. Even if the minor has a really good fake I.D. and a fully developed beard, the seller is still guilty for selling alcohol to *her*.

Transferred Intent

A final note about *mens rea* is that intent can be transferred. For instance, let's suppose you fire a gun at Mr. Quick and instead hit Mr. Slow.

In this case, your intent to kill Mr. Quick will be "transferred" to Mr. Slow. Also, in addition to being charged with the murder of Mr. Slow, you will be charged with the attempted murder of Mr. Quick. The lesson here is simple: When at all possible, shoot from

point blank range so you don't miss!

NOTE FROM THE PUBLISHER: Yes, he is kidding. Neither the author, the publisher nor the printer of this book condones shooting anyone at *any* time. Unfortunately, we cannot speak for the U.S. Postal Service in this regard.

CATEGORIES OF CRIMES

There are three categories of crimes:

(1) felonies;

(2) misdemeanors; and

(3) infractions.

Felonies are serious crimes punishable by imprisonment, unless you are a celebrity or a former President. Misdemeanors are lesser crimes that carry limited jail time (usually no more than six months). Infractions are technical violations of the law, such as the failure to timely renew your driver's license. Infractions are punished even less severely than misdemeanors, unless that infraction is forgetting your wedding anniversary *again*.

Chapter in Review
Elements of a Crime

1. **What is "mens rea"?**

    a. A person's mental state

    b. "That time of the month"

    c. What happens to you after eating my wife's meatloaf

2. **What is malice?**

    a. Specific intent to cause a certain harm

    b. The secret love child of Mel and Alice on the TV show, *Alice*

    c. Reckless disregard to the danger caused by one's actions

3. **Which of the following is true about a misdemeanor?**

    a. It's an unmarried female demeanor

    b. It's punished *less* severely than a felony

    c. It's like sex; the more I miss it, the meaner I get

Chapter 21

CRIMES AGAINST THE PERSON
That Dreaded Third Strike

NOTE FROM THE AUTHOR: Please note that if you are currently studying to be a criminal, you will want to concentrate on the crimes listed in the *next* chapter. Each of the crimes in this chapter is a violent crime. In most cases, a conviction for a violent crime will result in your *long-term* commitment to a loving relationship with "Bubba."

BATTERY

Battery is unlawfully touching another person. In this context, touching is unlawful if it either causes injury or is offensive. Therefore, punching, grabbing or spitting at someone would constitute battery.

Of course, touching is only unlawful if it is done without the *touchee's* consent. Therefore, Mistress Helga of the Imperial Dungeon is not guilty of battery (although I still think that her hourly rate of $300 is *criminal*).

ASSAULT

Assault is attempted battery. Therefore, throwing a punch at someone is assault, even if "they were just asking for it."

Also, causing fear of an immediate battery is assault. For instance, if the offender moves in a threatening manner, causing the victim to flinch, then he has committed assault. This is true even if the *flincher* (the

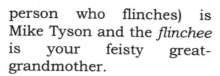

Things That Really Should Be Crimes

1. Ordering five cheeseburgers, four orders of fries, two apple pastries, a vanilla shake and a *diet* soda from a fast food restaurant

2. Wearing hair rollers, a shower cap or slippers outside of your house

3. Wearing black dress socks and sandals with short pants

4. Exposing an innocent family to "plumber's crack"

5. Forwarding chain e-mails

person who flinches) is Mike Tyson and the *flinchee* is your feisty great-grandmother.

Aggravated assault is a more severe form of assault, such as assault with a deadly weapon, assault with the intent to commit murder, or leaving the toilet seat up.

FALSE IMPRISONMENT AND KIDNAPPING

False imprisonment is unlawfully confining someone against his will. The key term here is "confining." In this context, confinement means restricting the victim's movement in *all* directions.

For instance, the local bar bouncer is not guilty of false imprisonment because he throws you out of the bar and blocks your re-entry. After all, you are free to move in any other direction. This is true even if you were wrongfully ejected from the bar after having *only* 16 beers.

Kidnapping is similar to false imprisonment but it also requires that you move the victim. For instance, let's suppose you invite your boss over for dinner. To ensure that you make a good impression, you lock your crazy Uncle Lester in the attic. This is false imprisonment.

However, let's assume that you really don't want

to take any chances and therefore, you lock Uncle Lester in your neighbor's attic. In this case, you have committed the crime of kidnapping.

SEX CRIMES

Rape

Rape is sexual intercourse with a woman *without her consent*. Historically, a married woman was legally presumed to consent to sex with her husband at *all* times. As a result, a husband couldn't be convicted of raping his wife. Sadly, until the late 1970s, some states still followed this view. Currently, spousal rape is a crime in all 50 states.

In order to gain a rape conviction, the prosecution must not only prove that the victim did not consent to sexual intercourse but also, that the offender knew or should have known that the victim did not consent. If the defendant honestly and reasonably believed that the victim consented to sex, then he is not guilty of rape.

As a result, the victim is frequently "placed on trial." A defendant will often argue that based on the victim's actions, he had an honest and reasonable belief that the victim had consented to sex.

Statutory Rape

However, consent is not an issue in statutory rape cases. Statutory rape laws make it illegal to engage in sexual intercourse with a female younger than some specified age (e.g., 16 or 18). As a matter of law, a female younger than this age cannot consent to sexual intercourse. In most states, the offender will not be excused even if he had good reason to believe that the female was of lawful age.

Consensual Sex Crimes

Even some forms of consensual sex are illegal. For instance, in some states, adultery is a crime punishable by imprisonment, fine or alimony. Likewise, sodomy is banned in many states. Fornication, which is defined as sex between people who are not married to *each other* (i.e., "good sex"), is a crime in other states.

Finally, some states treat

seduction as a crime. The crime of seduction occurs when a man convinces a woman to engage in sexual intercourse by falsely promising to marry her. However, it is not a crime to convince a woman to sleep with you by exaggerating about how much you really respect her for her mind.

HOMICIDE

A *homicide* can be most easily defined as the killing of a human being. However, depending upon the manner and the intent of the killer, the punishment can vary significantly. In general, homicide is broken into three classes:

(1) murder;

(2) voluntary manslaughter; and

(3) involuntary manslaughter.

Murder

A murder is a homicide committed with *malice*. In this case, malice is the intent to kill, intent to seriously injure, or reckless disregard for human life.

Malice is also demonstrated when the homicide occurs during the commis-

sion of another felony. This is the so-called "felony-murder rule."

The most obvious example of a "felony-murder" homicide is an armed bank robbery that turns into a shoot-out. In this situation, the bank robber can be charged with murder if anyone dies in the shoot-out. Also, the robber's bank will charge him the standard fee of $1.50 for not using the ATM.

The "felony-murder" rule only applies in the case of a dangerous felony. Therefore, the "felony-murder" rule never applies to deaths that result from perjury, tax evasion or tearing the tag off your mattress.

Murder is classified into degrees. In many states, first-degree murder includes premeditated murder. Also, certain felony-murders are classified as first degree murders.

First degree murder also includes murder by torture and other cruel methods, such as forcing the victim to listen to John Tesh albums. However, if the killing wasn't planned, torturous, or a part of another

felony, then it will be qualified as second degree in most states.

Voluntary Manslaughter

In some circumstances, second degree murder will be reduced to voluntary manslaughter. One such circumstance is when the offender has been *adequately provoked*. Of course, in these cases, the provocation must be severe. Therefore, a wife can't legally kill her husband just because he admits that she looks fat in a particular dress (as a general rule of thumb, ladies, if you have to ask, then you do). Although a wife may pout and mope around the house until her husband wishes he were dead.

Also, the offender must have been provoked *by the victim* and not some other person. Therefore, ladies, it isn't legal to kill your new boyfriend because your old boyfriend was a jerk.

Also, the killing must occur in the "heat of passion" (i.e., within a short time after the provocation). Therefore, you can't hunt down the motorist who cut you off in traffic six months ago. However, the driver who cuts you off today is fair game, especially if you live in Los Angeles.

The classic example of reasonable provocation is when a husband arrives home to find his wife in bed with another man. In this situation, if the husband kills either of them in the "heat of passion," he may be charged with voluntary manslaughter instead of second degree murder.

In a few states, murder can be reduced to voluntary manslaughter if the offender has *diminished capacity*. Diminished capacity is a mental defect that doesn't quite meet the standard of legal insanity. For instance, in some cases, a person intoxicated by alcohol or drugs has diminished capacity. However, plain stupidity *never* qualifies as diminished capacity as it is far too common among criminals.

Involuntary Manslaughter

Involuntary manslaughter is a homicide that was not committed maliciously. Therefore, if the offender commits a homicide while only attempting to slightly injure the victim, he is guilty of involuntary manslaughter and not murder.

For instance, let's suppose Spitball Sammy is shooting spitballs in school one day. Sammy spots his favorite target, Humpty Dumpty, sitting on a wall. Sammy hits Humpty Dumpty with a spitball, causing a great fall. Unfortunately, all of the king's horses and all of the king's men couldn't put Humpty Dumpty back together again.

In this case, Sammy is guilty of involuntary *egg*-slaughter. And, of course, Humpty Dumpty's parents will sue the school district, the king, his horses and his men.

Also, an offender may be found guilty of involuntary manslaughter if she acted

with criminal negligence. Criminal negligence is conduct that creates a *serious* risk of death or bodily injury. Obviously, driving 5 MPH over the speed limit is not criminal negligence. However, driving 25 MPH over the speed limit *in reverse while blindfolded* is criminal negligence.

Finally, just as there is the felony-murder rule, there is the "misdemeanor-manslaughter rule." If someone causes a death while committing a misdemeanor, he is also guilty of involuntary manslaughter.

However, this rule only applies to misdemeanors that are morally wrong and not mere infractions of the law.

Therefore, a driver fleeing from the police could be found guilty of misdemeanor-manslaughter if someone is killed during the chase. However, a driver couldn't be found guilty of misdemeanor-manslaughter just because he was two weeks late in renewing his license. Besides, being forced to spend the next six months waiting in line at the motor vehicle registration office is punishment enough.

Chapter in Review
Crimes Against the Person

1. Which of the following is a criminal battery?

   a.   Eveready

   b.   Duracell

   c.   Beating the stuffing out of that annoying Energizer bunny

2. Generally, murder is classified into how many degrees?

   a.   2

   b.   98.6

   c.   360

3. Murder committed in the "heat of passion" may be reduced to:

   a.   Second degree murder

   b.   Voluntary manslaughter

   c.   A 2-hour movie on The Lifetime Channel

Chapter 22

CRIMES AGAINST PROPERTY
Sometimes Crime Does Pay

Crimes against property fall into three basic categories:

(1) bonehead crimes -- larceny, robbery, burglary and extortion;

(2) clever crimes -- larceny by trick, false pretenses, embezzlement and forgery; and

(3) destructive crimes -- arson and malicious mischief.

BONEHEAD CRIMES

Larceny

Larceny is taking someone else's property with the intent to keep it. Therefore, even if a woman *borrows* her best friend's dress without permission, she hasn't committed larceny so long as she intends to return it. However, if she later decides to keep the dress because it matches her eyes and doesn't make her look so "hippy," then she has committed larceny.

Also, if the offender takes the property intending to *replace* it with an identical piece of property, then he is not guilty of larceny. Of course, in this case, the property taken must not be irreplaceable, like a family heirloom or a kidney.

Interestingly enough, larceny can be committed by the *owner* of the property. For example, let's suppose you take your car to Frick & Frack Auto Mechanics for an oil change. You spend two hours in a tiny waiting area drinking coffee that tastes like dirty dishwater and reading a 1985 issue of *Sports Illustrated*. Frick then informs you that the work has been completed and the total charge will be $50,000. You rightfully refuse to pay and storm off threatening to call your lawyer.

Although you aren't obligated to pay $50,000 for an oil change (except in New York City), Frick & Frack would have a statutory mechanic's lien against your car for the true value of the oil change. Therefore, if you go back to Frick & Frack's that night and drive your car away using your spare key, then you have committed larceny in some states.

Nevertheless, in certain circumstances, you do have the right to enter someone else's land to retrieve your property. For instance, let's suppose you lent your lawn mower to a neighbor six *years* ago. In this case, you can walk onto his property and reclaim your lawn mower. This same principle allows the repoman to repossess your car.

However, please do not get carried away here! First of all, you can't use force to enter onto your neighbor's property. For instance, let's suppose you inadvertently leave your last pack of cigarettes in your neighbor's car. If your neighbor leaves his car door unlocked, then you may enter his car to retrieve your cigarettes. However, if the car door is locked, then you may not break the windows just to get to your cigarettes. And trust me, as a smoker, I truly understand the temptation.

Secondly, you can only enter someone's land to the extent necessary to reclaim your property. Therefore, you can't enter your neighbor's home to make long-distance phone calls and take a bubble bath just because your neighbor hasn't returned your property. This is the case even if the property borrowed is your *spouse*.

Finally, there are two forms of larceny – petty and grand. Most states define

"petty larceny" as larceny where the value of the property taken is less than some amount (e.g., $500). Grand larceny is larceny where the value of the property is greater than this amount.

Robbery

Robbery is similar to larceny, except in a robbery, the property is taken *by force.* For instance, a purse-snatcher is guilty of robbery. However, a skillful pickpocket doesn't use force to steal your property and therefore, he is only guilty of larceny.

Interestingly, threats are considered "force" for this purpose. However, the threat must be a threat of *immediate* physical injury. Threatening to harm someone in the future is not robbery, but extortion.

Extortion

Extortion is making a threat of future harm to obtain property. And the threat does not have to be a threat of bodily harm. For instance, if you demand your boss' Porsche in exchange for not telling his wife about Brandy from the office Christmas party, you are an extortionist. You are also being short-sighted because he may be willing to part with some cash as well.

Burglary

Historically, burglary was *breaking and entering* into a *dwelling house* to commit a crime inside. To satisfy the "breaking and entering" requirement, the offender had to open a door or window to enter the dwelling. An offender who walked into a house where the door had been left wide open did not "break and enter." This is no longer the case in many states.

Also, historically, the term "dwelling house" applied strictly to homes. However, under many current laws, burglary applies to any structure and, in some states, even cars and fenced-in areas.

Finally, the offender must enter the dwelling with the intent to commit some crime *inside.* Therefore, if the offender enters your home merely to have some porridge, sit in your chairs and sleep in your beds, then she has not committed burglary but

A Lawpsided View
Burglary

In October 2001, O.J. Simpson faced charges of battery and burglary in a Florida courtroom. These charges stemmed from a road rage incident. Although the precise facts of this case were in dispute, some facts were known.

On December 4, 2000, Simpson "allegedly" rolled through a stop sign. Another motorist, Jeffrey Pattinson, flashed his lights at Simpson. According to Simpson, Pattinson then proceeded to honk his horn, flash his headlights and tail Simpson for another 150 yards. On the other hand, Pattinson insisted that "I am rubber, you are glue, whatever you say, bounces off of me and sticks to you!"

In any event, Simpson pulled over and approached Pattinson's car and the two men "exchanged words." Then, remarkably, O.J. "allegedly" reached into Pattinson's car and snatched his eyeglasses, which, unfortunately for Pattinson, were still on his face.

Of course, even more remarkable to me is the fact that Pattinson chose to "exchange words" with O.J. Is the sanctity of the stop sign really that important to him? Was it important enough for him to go fist-to-nose with O.J. "It Must Have Been Colombian Drug Lords" Simpson? I don't think so. As far as I am concerned, O.J. Simpson *always* has the right of way.

In any event, Simpson was charged with battery and burglary. If convicted on both counts, he could have faced up to 16 *years* in prison. Yes, years! While the battery charge only carried a maximum sentence of one year, the burglary charge carried a maximum prison term of 15 years.

Under Florida law, a burglary is defined as "entering or remaining in a dwelling, a structure, or a conveyance with the intent to commit an offense therein." For those of you educated in our public school system, a "conveyance" is not a type of store where you can buy lottery tickets, cigarettes or *Slim Jims*. A conveyance is any vehicle that can be used to carry (or convey) passengers, such as a train, bus, boat, car, minivan or any vehicle other than an American car built in the 1970s.

As a result, Simpson was technically guilty of burglary. He did *enter* Pattinson's *conveyance* with the *intent* to commit the *crime* of battery. Nevertheless, I think the prosecution took this case too far.

After all, if this incident had occurred outside of the car, O.J. would have received a maximum of one year for simple battery. In fact, even felony battery, which involves horrible consequences, such as great bodily harm, permanent disability, permanent disfigurement or marriage, only carries a maximum sentence of 5 years.

Nevertheless, in the end, O.J. won an acquittal in this case, bringing his record in legal proceedings to two wins, one loss and one "no contest."

rather trespass. This is sometimes (but not very often) referred to as the "Goldilocks Defense."

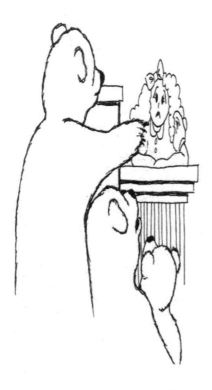

CLEVER CRIMES

Larceny by Trick and False Pretenses

Larceny by trick occurs when the offender tricks the victim into handing over his property. This occurs when a telemarketer claims that you have won $1 million in a contest that you never entered and requires you to "reserve" your prize with an initial deposit of $500. This is also called "larceny by stupidity."

False pretenses is when the offender tricks the victim into handing over *title* to the property rather than the actual property itself.

Embezzlement

Embezzlement occurs when the offender *converts* someone else's property for his own use. For instance, the bank teller who "converts" $500 from his money drawer into his pocket is guilty of embezzlement. Likewise, the corporate executive who "converts" $200,000,000 from her company's bank account into her Swiss bank account is guilty of embezzlement. The only difference between their crimes is that one of them has done a much better job of it. And who says crime doesn't pay?

Forgery

Forgery is making a false writing that has *legal significance*. The important thing to remember is that the writing must have legal significance. For instance, let's suppose Homely Herbert forges the following note and posts it in his cubicle at work:

Dear Herbert:

You were an animal last night! You are the best!

Hugs & Kisses,
Pamela Anderson

In this case, Herbert has not committed forgery because the note doesn't entitle him to anything of legal significance. The high-fiving and back-slapping from the guys in the mailroom isn't legally significant.

However, forging the following note would have legal significance and therefore, is a crime:

Dear Judy:

I would have nothing without your invaluable assistance. Please present this note to my bank so they can transfer $20 billion into your account.

Gratefully,

Bill Gates

Other Larcenies

1. **Larceny by Fraction** - This is how gas stations convince you that 99 9/10¢ per gallon is much cheaper than $1 per gallon.

2. **Larceny by Forgetfulness** - This is when a credit card company offers you a service that you never use. This service shows up as a charge on your statement every month but you always forget to cancel it.

3. **Larceny by Diet** - This is when you pay a health club $30 per month *for life* even though you haven't worked out there since 1983.

4. **Larceny by Rebate** - This is when you pay $200 more than a product is worth because you are entitled to a $200 rebate, which you never remember to send in.

5. **Larceny by Informercial** - This is when you are convinced at 3 a.m. that "You can get rich by placing *tiny* classified ads in the newspaper." So you pick up the phone "right now" and order the kit for just "3 easy payments of $69.99" (see also *Larceny by Fraction*).

6. **Larceny by Expense Account** – This is when you charge X-rated movies and items from the hotel gift shop to your hotel room and then submit the bill for reimbursement to your employer (hypothetically speaking, of course).

7. **Larceny by Overtime** – This is when you work late and use your employer's computer, photocopier and supplies to produce and distribute your legal humor book without sharing a dime of the $14.95 cover price (once again, hypothetically speaking, of course).

DESTRUCTIVE CRIMES

Arson and Malicious Mischief

Historically, arson was defined as burning *someone else's* dwelling house. However, the term "dwelling house" has expanded over the years. It now includes just about any structure. Also, most arson statutes make it a crime to burn down your own home, particularly if you do so to collect the insurance money.

Interestingly, in some states, arson requires actual fire damage to the structure. Smoke damage by itself is not enough. Therefore, a group of men playing poker are not guilty of arson regardless of the number of cigars they smoke. Of course, this assumes that they are not smoking cigars in California, where smoking is punishable by death.

Maliciously destroying or damaging someone else's property is malicious mischief. If you have further questions about this crime, then simply observe your children. If they are anything like mine, they are experts at it.

Chapter in Review
Crimes Against Property

1. **What is petty larceny?**
    a. How Tom Petty has supported himself since his band broke up
    b. Theft of the Mona Lisa
    c. Theft of my 1967 Pinto

2. **For a false writing to constitute a forgery, it must:**
    a. Be written in ink
    b. Have legal significance
    c. What was the question again?

3. **What is larceny by trick?**
    a. What happened to Hugh Grant on Sunset Boulevard
    b. How little kids in costumes convince you to give them candy on Halloween
    c. Any transaction involving a used car salesman

Chapter 23

INCHOATE CRIMES
When You're Too Much of a Wimp to Do It Yourself

An *inchoate* (pronounced inkówät) crime is a crime that leads to another crime. Examples of inchoate crimes are:

- **Conspiracies**
- **Attempts**
- **Solicitation**

CONSPIRACY

A conspiracy occurs when two or more people agree to commit some illegal act. The key element of this crime is the agreement itself. Obviously, the agreement need not be written or spelled out in great detail. After all, much like Dan Quayle, criminals are not known for their spelling prowess.

However, there must be some agreement between the offenders. For example, if two strangers *independently* break into the same warehouse on the same evening, they have not *conspired* to commit burglary.

Also, each conspirator must intend to achieve a criminal objective. For instance, let's suppose two employees, Oscar and Felix, *agree* to confront their boss about his abusive behavior. Without Felix's knowledge, Oscar decides to express his grievances by hitting the boss over the head with a hammer. In this case, there has been no conspiracy to commit battery.

In addition to the agreement, there must be at least one act committed in furtherance of the conspiracy. For instance, let's suppose the neighborhood kids decide to toilet-paper the house of Old Lady Jeffreys. The criminal conspiracy does not start until one of them goes to Costco and buys the ridiculous 128-roll package of toilet paper for $1.99.

At law, *each* conspirator is responsible for all crimes committed in furtherance of the conspiracy. Therefore, if there is a conspiracy to rob a bank, *each* conspirator will be responsible for all crimes committed -- the theft of the get-away car, the bank robbery itself and the illegal parking outside the bank. In addition, conspiracy is a crime punishable in and of itself.

ATTEMPTS

To be guilty of an attempt, the offender must have specific intent to commit the crime. For example, there is no such thing as "attempted involuntary manslaughter."

Also, the offender must have committed at least one "act of *perpetration*." This is a higher threshold than the act required for the crime of conspiracy, which is an "act of *preparation*." The act of perpetration must be a *substantial* step toward committing the crime.

This is hard to define precisely, but it is clear that if the offender has committed the last act necessary for completion of the crime, she has committed an "act of perpetration." For instance, mixing rat poison in your boss' coffee mug and serving it to him is clearly an "act of perpetration." On the other hand, merely buying the rat poison is not an act of perpetration.

SOLICITATION

Solicitation is inciting, commanding, or requesting another person to commit a crime. Unlike conspiracy, solicitation doesn't require agreement. The crime is committed when the solicitation is made, even if rejected immediately.

ACCOMPLICES

Accomplices can be broken down into three categories:

(1) **principals in the second degree;**

(2) **accessories before the fact; and**

(3) **accessories after the fact.**

Principal in the Second Degree

A principal in the second degree is a person who is present at the scene of the crime and aids the offender. For instance, let's suppose I buy my wife a frying pan for our anniversary. After all, I am nothing if not romantic. After opening her "gift," she uses it to bash me over the head.

Of course, in this case, I am <u>not</u> a principal in the second degree to my own assault because I had no reason to believe this would happen. On second thought, maybe I did.

Accessory Before the Fact

An accessory before the fact is someone who aids another person to commit a crime but is not present at the scene of the crime. Of course, this person must have *intended* to aid the crime.

For instance, let's suppose MacGyver walks into a convenience store and places a package of Twinkies, a bottle of mineral water and a Slim Jim on the counter. The clerk rings up his purchase and MacGyver leaves the store.

MacGyver then uses these seemingly innocuous items to create a deadly weapon, which he uses on the people who cancelled his show. In this case, although the convenience store clerk aided MacGyver by ringing up his order, the clerk will not be charged as an accessory before the fact.

Accessory After the Fact

As a general rule, you don't have a duty to help the police to find criminals.

On the other hand, you can't help a criminal to avoid capture either. If you do, then you may be charged with being an accessory after the fact.

For instance, if I see my brother-in-law on *America's Most Wanted* (and it's just a matter of time), I can't call and warn him. This not only would be illegal but also, impossible, as his telephone service has been disconnected since I've known him.

Nevertheless, assuming that I become an accessory after the fact, I will only be punished for this crime. I won't be punished for his numerous other crimes, the biggest of which was marrying my little sister.

This is not the case with the other accessory crimes. A principal in the second degree or an accessory before the fact can be punished for the crimes of the offender.

Chapter in Review
Inchoate Crimes

1. A criminal conspiracy requires which of the following?

   a. Agreement among offenders to commit an illegal act

   b. Oliver Stone to make a 6-hour movie about it

   c. Right-wing conservatives

2. An attempt crime requires:

   a. An act of preparation

   b. Preparation H

   c. An act of perpetration

3. Which accessories are held responsible for the crimes of the principal?

   a. Belts, earrings and purses

   b. The Vice Principal

   c. Accessories before the fact

Chapter 24

DEFENSES
Beating the Rap

Even if you commit a crime, you may still avoid prison (and Bubba) if you have a defense available to you. Defenses come in two forms:

- **Justifications** - "Your Honor, he deserved a killing"; and

- **Excuses** - "The devil made me do it".

Justifications differ from excuses in that justifications provide a total defense against all punishment. On the other hand, although a valid excuse may keep you from going to prison, it won't protect you from other forms of punishment, such as commitment to a mental institution or a guest appearance on *The Jerry Springer Show*.

JUSTIFICATIONS

Self-Defense

A person may justifiably commit any number of crimes, including homicide, if he does so in self-defense. However, the self-defense justification is limited.

For one, the victim must have initiated the attack. Moreover, the attack must be a deadly attack. Therefore, you can't respond to a kick in the shin by shooting the victim. This is true even in Texas (although I understand that "Kick Me and I'll Shoot You" legislation is currently pending).

Also, self-defense can't be used to retaliate once the "deadly attack" has ended. In other words, once the bad guy runs out of bullets, you can no longer shoot him.

Also, deadly force may be used only when *absolutely necessary* to defend yourself. Therefore, Jean Claude Van Damme can't shoot a little old lady who attacks him with a rusty nail file. After all, he could easily subdue her by delivering a well-placed kick or making her watch one of his movies.

In some states, the defendant has the additional burden of proving that he *had* to fight. If the defendant could have run away, then the self-defense justification is not available to him.

The self-defense justification can be used to defend others as well. The defendant need not have a special relationship with the person whom he is defending. However, the defendant can only defend the person who would have had

the right to self-defense in the first place.

For instance, let's suppose Gentlemanly George is driving through Beverly Hills and sees Zsa Zsa Gabor engaged in a fist fight with a male police officer. Being a gentleman, he pulls over and renders assistance to a "damsel in distress" by beating up the police officer. In this case, if Zsa Zsa started the fight (which is likely), then Greg's actions aren't justified.

Lastly, you may use deadly force to prevent an intruder from entering your home. However, in many states, you may not use deadly force to prevent an intruder from *leaving* your home. Therefore, you can't shoot a burglar as he *leaves* your home, even if he is getting away with your jewelry, TV set or worse, your beer.

Self-Defense in Action

Prosecutor: "You claim that the victim came at you with a broken bottle in his hand. But is it not true, that you had something in your hand as well?

Defendant: "Yes, his wife. Very charming, of course, but not much good in a fight."

Mistake

In some instances, the defendant makes an honest mistake. He thinks his actions are justified but, in reality, they are not. In these cases, the defendant may still avoid punishment if he had an honest and reasonable belief that his actions were justified.

For instance, let's suppose Cheesy Chester is in a crowded bar one night when he hears what he believes to be gunshots. In an act of "heroism," Chester tackles a complete stranger, Lovely Linda, and pins her to the floor to shield her from the bullets. It is discovered later that the gunshot sounds came from the bar's television set.

In this case, Chester has technically committed an unjustified battery against Linda. However, if Chester's mistake was in good faith and reasonable, then his battery will be excused.

NOTE FROM THE AUTHOR: Guys, please do not get any "brilliant" ideas here! You can't use this as a new "pick-up" device. Trust me on this one.

Preventing a Greater Harm

In some cases, a crime may be justified if it prevents a greater harm to society. For instance, a person would be justified in breaking a store window in order to get a fire extinguisher to put out a fire.

However, on the other hand, you can't pollute your neighborhood with insecticides just because you find *one* ant in your house. Unless, of course, it is my *Aunt* Trudy, in which case, you are legally allowed to "do what you've got to do."

Likewise, you can lawfully commit *any* crime to prevent N'Sync from coming out with another album. As you can see, it all depends on the severity of the harm to be avoided.

EXCUSES

Excuses are used to demonstrate that the defendant did not have the requisite mental state to commit the crime.

Insanity

One excuse is the infamous "insanity defense." The test for insanity in most states is the *M'Naughten Rule*. Under this rule, a crime is excused if the defendant suffered from a mental disease that prevented him from knowing that his actions were wrong. If the defendant is found "not guilty by reason of insanity," he still may be committed to a mental institution until some undetermined future date. For those of you who have seen *One Flew Over the Cuckoo's Nest* (or have been to one of your spouse's family reunions), you know that joining Bubba in the state penitentiary may be preferable.

Some states allow for the excuse of *temporary insanity*. If the defendant is found "not guilty by reason of temporary insanity," he may be allowed to go free. As a result, temporary insanity defenses are rarely successful, much like people who major in Art History in college.

Intoxication

Another excuse used by offenders is intoxication. However, to be used as an excuse, the defendant must not have become intoxicated *voluntarily*. Therefore, if the defendant voluntarily ingests liquor or narcotics, he is voluntarily intoxicated.

On the other hand, involuntary intoxication occurs when the offender takes a substance not knowing that it is intoxicating (e.g., he eats my wife's cooking). Involuntary intoxication may excuse a number of crimes, even murder.

Finally, although voluntary intoxication will not excuse a crime, it may prevent the defendant from forming the *mens rea* necessary to commit the crime in the first place. For instance, voluntary intoxication may serve as an excuse for a crime that requires *specific* intent, such as attempted murder.

However, voluntary intoxication won't prevent your friends from teasing you for *attempting* to pick up a really ugly person in a bar. Even the law has its limits.

Age

A minor offender may use the "he's just a baby" excuse. Historically, the law treated children under a certain age (e.g., 7 years old) as legally incapable of forming the *mens rea* necessary for *any* crime. Children less than another age (e.g., 14 years old) were presumed to be likewise incapable but this presumption could be overcome with evidence.

Today, in most states, juvenile offenders are processed through a separate system and under rules that vary from state to state. In many states, juveniles are punished as adults for serious crimes. In other states, the juvenile offender is simply given a "timeout."

Entrapment

Entrapment occurs when the criminal plan is engineered by the police officer and the offender was not *predisposed* to commit the crime in the first place. Entrapment is very difficult to prove. For one, the officer must solicit the crime. In addition, the offender must prove that he was not predisposed to commit the crime anyway.

As an example, let's suppose our friend, Cheesy Chester, is cruising down Sunset Boulevard one evening. He is flagged down by the very sexy Roxanne. She makes an offer of prostitution and after some discussion, Chester agrees. However, Roxanne turns out to be an undercover police officer and arrests Chester for solicitation of prostitution.

In this case, Chester can use the entrapment defense only if he can prove that he was not predisposed to soliciting prostitution. Therefore, if he can show that he was on his way to a bible study meeting at his grandmother's nursing home, he may be excused. On the other hand, if he was driving back and forth down the boulevard on a Friday night, then he is in trouble.

Duress

If the offender is coerced into committing a crime, he may be excused by reason of duress. For instance, if someone forcibly wraps your hand around a gun and causes you to pull the trigger, you will not be punished for the shooting.

However, it is less clear when dealing with coercion by *threats* of physical force. For instance, let's suppose you are threatened that you will be killed unless you

shoot another person. In some states, this duress would excuse your crime. In other states, you would not be excused. In these states, you are *legally* required to choose your own death rather than kill another. Of course, this situation is extremely far-fetched and never presents itself, except in law school textbooks, prison or the Middle East.

In other cases of duress, the judge will compare the harm threatened against the harm done to the victim. The crime will be excused if the harm threatened outweighs the harm done.

For instance, let's suppose Immature Ivan wants to be accepted by "the guys." The guys ask Ivan to help them rob a convenience store. Ivan initially refuses but is threatened that he will be called a "chicken" if he doesn't help. Feeling peer pressure, Ivan participates in the robbery. When caught, Ivan won't be able to use duress as an excuse. The harm of being called a "chicken" doesn't outweigh the danger of a robbery.

Ineffective Excuses

The following excuses were never effective with our parents, nor are they effective in a court of law:

1. "Everybody's doing it."

2. "He started it!"

3. "He dared me to do it."

4. "My stomach hurts."

5. "My dog ate my homework."

Consent

The victim's consent will excuse some minor crimes but it won't excuse a felony. This is because felonies are not only crimes against the victim but crimes against society as well. In fact, in most cases, the government will prosecute the offender even if the victim refuses to press charges.

This explains why Dr. Jack Kervorkian was continually prosecuted and eventually convicted of murder, even though he had the consent of his "victims." However, this does not explain Kervorkian's bad hair cut and poor choice of wardrobe.

Chapter in Review
Defenses

1. The most common test for criminal insanity is:
   a. The Rorschach Test
   b. The Horshack Test
   c. The M'Naughten Rule

2. A successful entrapment defense requires:
   a. A defendant who was not "predisposed" to commit the crime
   b. A team of lawyers more costly than Johnny Carson's last divorce
   c. Really gullible jurors

3. Felonies are considered to be crimes against:
   a. Cats
   b. Nature
   c. Society

Chapter 25

PROCEDURAL REQUIREMENTS
Getting Off on a Technicality

In some cases, the defendant is guilty of a crime based on the evidence but found "not guilty" due to a technicality. A "technicality" is a legal requirement placed on police officers, lawyers and judges. These requirements are imposed to protect the constitutional rights of the defendant.

In short, our system is based upon the premise that it is better for 1,000 guilty people to go free than for one innocent person to be falsely imprisoned. This chapter illustrates how to become one of those 1,000 guilty people.

THE CONSTITUTION

Before discussing the technicalities in detail, it is important to point out that most of them are rooted in the first ten amendments to our Constitution, the Bill of Rights. The Bill of Rights was originally drafted to prevent the *federal* government from infringing upon the rights of the people. The 14th Amendment made these restrictions applicable to state governments as well.

UNREASONABLE SEIZURES

The Fourth Amendment to the Constitution prevents the police from making *unreasonable* seizures. As a result, police officers are limited in their ability to conduct searches, make arrests or seize a citizen's property, unless the property in question is a suspicious-looking jelly donut.

Arrests

To make a lawful arrest, a police officer must have either *probable cause* or a valid arrest warrant. Probable cause is a reasonable belief that the suspect has committed the crime. Based on probable cause, a police officer can make an arrest for a felony. However, unless the officer actually witnessed the crime, she must obtain a warrant *prior* to an arrest for a misdemeanor.

Stop and Frisk

A police officer does not need probable cause to merely stop a suspect on the street. To stop a suspect, the police officer only needs to be able to articulate an *objective* basis for suspicion. This is the so-called "reasonable belief" test. In this context, reasonable belief must be more substantial than "he had beady eyes" but not much more.

Once an officer has made a lawful stop, he can demand identification from the suspect. Also, he can frisk the suspect for weapons if he has a reasonable belief that the suspect is armed, intoxicated or African-American. Lastly, the officer may frisk any suspect whom he finds physically attractive (thus, the

term "to *cop* a feel").

Traffic Stops

Police officers must have a reasonable belief that an infraction has occurred before making a traffic stop. The only exception to this rule is in the case of random drunk driving and immigration checkpoint stops. However, even in these cases, the stops must be made according to a set formula (e.g., every fifth car).

UNREASONABLE SEARCHES

In making a case for trial, police officers must often conduct investigations to find evidence of the suspect's guilt. These investigations often result in searches of the suspect's home or other property. Each of these searches is subject to the Fourth Amendment's restriction against *"unreasonable searches* of persons, houses, papers, and effects."

Of course, the questions remain: "What is a "search"? "When does it become unreasonable"? "Why didn't I go to Business School instead?"

A *Lawsided* View
Random Drug Checkpoints

In November 2000, the Supreme Court ruled that random drug checkpoints violated citizens' reasonable expectations of privacy in their cars and therefore, were unconstitutional under the Fourth Amendment. The case involved the Indianapolis Police Department's practice of roadblocks and random stops over a four-month period in 1998.

Although I am not a legal scholar, I must respect-fully disagree with the Court's decision in this case. First, I challenge the Court's premise that people have a reasonable expectation of privacy in their cars. For instance, if you park your car in my neighborhood, you don't even have a reasonable expectation that it will be there when you get back.

Of course, I will concede that many people have expectations of privacy in their cars. However, I contend that these expectations are "unreasonable." This explains why some people pick their noses while driving, as if their windows were made of one-way glass. This also explains why others play music loud enough to affect the rotational spin of the planet and why millions of people bought American cars during the 1970s and *expected* them to run. As you can see, we have many unreasonable expectations regarding auto-mobiles.

Furthermore, the Court's decision in this case was inconsistent with prior decisions involving sobriety checkpoints. The Supreme Court has upheld sobriety checkpoints because getting drunk drivers off the road actually saves lives. However, are crack drivers somehow safer than drunk drivers? Or does the Court believe that a crack addict will actually wait until he gets home before lighting up? Oh please! I can't even make it home from McDonald's before I start digging into the French fries and I'm not addicted to them (well, not very addicted).

This ruling is also inconsistent with the high court's ruling on immigration checkpoint stops. Is the U.S. Supreme Court taking the position that illegal immigration is more dangerous than the illegal drug trade? Please! Illegal immigrants are not responsible for any of the crime, disease and poverty attributable to drug addicts. Moreover, a drug addict isn't going to paint your entire house, mow your lawn and watch your kids for $50/week either.

In fact, I find it hard to believe that the justices on the Court are really this naïve. Perhaps they are using drugs themselves. After all, we don't call them the "high" court for nothing. In fact, that would possibly explain some of their recent rulings.

Or maybe they are dealing drugs in an effort to supplement their meager $180,000 annual salaries. In any event, I think we need to investigate. Where is Ken Starr when we need him?

What is a Search?

Over the years, the courts have decided that a search occurs when the police intrude upon the suspect's *reasonable expectation of privacy*. As a matter of law, each of us has a reasonable expectation of privacy in our homes, unless, of course, we have children.

However, we do not have a reasonable expectation of privacy for evidence that is in the plain view of the investigating officer. For instance, let's suppose Drug-dealing Derrick grows marijuana plants in his home. Derrick grows the plants in a large bay window visible from the street. In this case, Derrick does not have a reasonable expectation of privacy with respect to the marijuana in his home.

Nor is there a *reasonable expectation of privacy* for secrets told to a friend. If you've ever seen a daytime TV talk show, you'd have to agree on this point.

Also, if the suspect consents to the search, then he waives his *reasonable expectation of privacy*. Interestingly, many people do not realize that they have

the right to refuse consent to a police search. As a result, they unknowingly give up their constitutional rights.

For instance, each week on the TV show, *Cops*, a shirtless, toothless motorist consents to a search of his car, despite the fact that he has three *tons* of cocaine overflowing from his trunk.

In this case, the intelligent course of action is to withhold your consent to the search. In truth, this is probably the smart thing to do, even if you have nothing to hide. If the police officer insists upon conducting the search anyway, you have at least preserved your right to challenge it in court.

WARNING: Even if you feel the search is illegal, DO NOT INTERFERE WITH THE POLICE OFFICER CONDUCTING THE SEARCH! I am serious here! In court, you will have an opportunity to make your case but on the street, the police officer has the last word. He has a big stick *and* a gun, both of which he is empowered by law to use on *you*. In the immortal words of Rodney King, "Ouch! Ouch! Hey, stop hitting me!"

Also, please note that your reasonable expectation of privacy only applies to *governmental* searches. The Fourth Amendment doesn't protect you from the actions of private individuals, such as your parents, roommates or that nosy neighbor down the street. And, of course, any married man knows that the Fourth Amendment doesn't protect him from unreasonable searches and seizures by his wife.

Is the Search Reasonable?

Now, let's assume the police investigation is con-sidered a search. The question then turns to whether the search was reasonable. To be reasonable, the search must be based upon a valid search warrant or *probable cause*.

Search warrants are written out by magistrates, who have a wide range of discretion in deciding whether to issue search warrants. However, the magistrate must be neutral and detached from the criminal investigation. Therefore, the magistrate can't be the lead investigator of the crime. Of course, this sometimes presents problems in small towns, where the magistrate is usually also the Justice of the Peace, tavern keeper, TV anchorperson, midwife and greeter at Wal-Mart.

Also, a valid search warrant describes the place to be searched and the items to be seized. This limits the scope of the search to prevent officers from searching through a woman's panty drawer while supposedly looking for a *car* she is accused of stealing.

And even if there is no valid search warrant, the

search still may be reasonable if it is conducted with *probable cause*. For instance, if a search was conducted while frisking, arresting, or booking the suspect, then it was conducted with probable cause.

In these cases, police may also search the immediate area to ensure that the suspect doesn't have access to weapons. Critics often complain that police officers use this rule to extend their searches unjustifiably. Police officers often respond to this criticism with a nightstick to the head of the critic.

The Exclusionary Rule

Now, let's suppose a court determines that the police have conducted an unreasonable search. What happens then? Interestingly, the Fourth Amendment doesn't specifically address this issue. It simply prohibits unreasonable searches. It doesn't state what happens if an unreasonable search is conducted.

However, over the last century, the Supreme Court has created its own remedy. If the police conduct an un-

reasonable search, then the evidence uncovered in the search will be excluded from trial. This is the so-called "exclusionary rule."

In fact, not only is the illegally-seized evidence excluded but also, all future evidence obtained as a result. The exclusion of all further evidence is called the "fruit of the poisonous tree" doctrine.

For example, let's suppose the police illegally search the home of a suspected bookie. During the search, they find a list of names, phone numbers and bets taken by the suspect. The police then make contact with the people on the list and many of them provide valuable information. However, because of the "exclusionary rule" and the "fruit of the poisonous tree" doctrine, this evidence will be excluded at trial.

Interestingly, this evidence will be excluded only in the trial of the suspected bookie. If the customers are charged with crimes, the exclusionary rule won't be available to them. Only the person whose rights are violated can claim protection under the Fourth Amendment.

NOTE FROM THE AUTHOR: The end result of the exclusionary rule is that judges regularly free offenders who otherwise would have been proven guilty of violent crimes. In many cases, these same suspects return to the streets to commit even more violent crimes. I just wanted to point out the costs of civil liberty because freedom sure ain't free.

SELF-INCRIMINATION

In addition to uncovering physical evidence, police officers and prosecutors often seek a confession from the suspect. The Fifth Amendment to the Constitution establishes that no person "shall be compelled ... to be a witness against himself."

As a result, the suspect has the right to remain silent after being taken into custody and must be informed of this right prior to any questioning. The officer informs the suspect of this right by reciting these now famous words:

"You have the right to remain silent. Anything you say can, and will, be used against you in a court of law. You have the right to an attorney and to have that attorney present during questioning. If you cannot afford an attorney, we will provide you with the dumbest lawyer we can find!"

This warning is called the *Miranda* warning. If the police fail to give this warning, then *all* statements made during interrogation are inadmissible at trial.

Also, the Fifth Amendment protects defendants from being forced to testify at trial. Of course, the defendant is free to testify if he wishes.

RIGHT TO COUNSEL

One of a defendant's fundamental rights is the Sixth Amendment right to legal counsel. This right is so fundamental that counsel will be provided for free if the accused can't afford a lawyer. Of course, you usually get what you pay for in life. Therefore, your court-appointed lawyer is likely to be about as effective as the "rhythm method," only less enjoyable for all concerned.

However, the state must provide counsel only when the defendant faces imprisonment.   Therefore, you have no right to a court-appointed lawyer to fight a traffic ticket.   Unless, of course, you happen to drive like James Brown.

If court-appointed counsel is mandated, then the counsel must be *effective.* In fact, a conviction can be reversed if the accused was ineffectively represented at trial.

Obviously, to be effective, the lawyer must be involved early enough in the proceeding.   For instance, if the state waits until closing arguments to appoint counsel for the accused, then counsel won't be effective at that point.

As a result, lawyers are required in the earliest stages of the process – the bail hearing, the preliminary hearing, the appearance on *Larry King Live*, etc. In fact, lawyers are even required, in some cases, for police lineups.

The theory is that the presence of a suspect's lawyer will ensure that the police don't coach the witness or otherwise influence the process. In any event, the presence of a lawyer will certainly increase the suspect's legal bill.

Of course, at this point, you may be thinking that the best strategy for a defendant is to choose the most incompetent lawyer he can find for trial (any government lawyer will do nicely). In this case, if he loses at trial, then he can claim ineffective counsel. However, reversing a conviction on appeal is much like loving your spouse "til death do you part" (i.e., it's much easier said than done).

Courts are reluctant to overturn jury verdicts on this basis. They do so only when the defendant proves that there was a reasonable probability that the outcome of the trial would have been different if not for his attorney's *specific* errors. This is a fairly high standard to meet.

As a rule, judges presume that the actions of the defense attorney were sound trial strategy unless it can be conclusively proven otherwise. Therefore, even if your attorney calls your ex-girlfriend to the stand as a character witness, your conviction will probably not be overturned on appeal.

When convictions are overturned, it's usually because of some *egregious* error in the process, such as the state appointing the *victim's brother* as the defendant's attorney.

THE TRIAL PROCESS

The Bail Hearing

In felony cases, the first court appearance for the defendant is the bail hearing. The Eighth Amendment states that "excessive bail shall not be required." Bail is excessive if it exceeds the amount necessary to ensure that the accused will stick around for the trial. As a general rule, bail is higher when the nature of the crime is more serious or when the accused is likely to jump into a Ford Bronco with a gun, fake beard, passport and thousands of dollars in cash.

The Indictment

In federal cases, before

Warning Signs That You Have "Ineffective Counsel"

1. Your lawyer thinks the "fruit of the poisonous tree doctrine" was first introduced in Snow White and the Seven Dwarfs.

2. Your lawyer addresses the jury by saying, "So you are the twelve losers who weren't smart enough to get out of jury duty, huh?"

3. Your lawyer thinks the "exclusionary rule" is the reason there are so few black hockey players.

4. Your lawyer continually mocks the judge about his robe and addresses him as "Your Sissiness."

5. Your lawyer passes the bar on the night before trial … and decides to stop in for a few.

going to trial, the prosecutor must first get an *indictment* from the grand jury. This indictment requirement also applies in some states.

An indictment is a declaration that there is enough evidence to pursue charges against the suspect. It is not a determination of guilt or innocence.

Also, a grand jury proceeding is different from a criminal trial in other respects. For one, the defendant is not allowed to put on a defense. The grand jury only judges the merits of the prosecution's case. If the prosecution presents evidence that, *if true,* would prove the defendant guilty, then the grand jury is instructed to "hand down" an indictment. This is a very easy hurdle for the prosecution to clear.

In fact, several critics have suggested that it's possible to get a grand jury to indict a ham sandwich for murder. Of course, this is ridiculous! There is only one reported case of a ham sandwich being indicted.

NOTE FROM THE AUTHOR: For the record, the ham sandwich was ac-

quitted of all charges at trial. However, its co-defendant, a bucket of fries, didn't fare so well.

The Preliminary Hearing

Some states do not require that the prosecution secure an indictment. In these states, the defendant goes straight to the *preliminary hearing.*

Unlike in a grand jury proceeding, in a preliminary hearing, the defendant has the right to cross-examine witnesses. The purpose of this hearing is to screen out cases that are shakier than Strom Thurmond performing neurosurgery.

Nevertheless, the same burden of proof applies in a preliminary hearing. Namely, the prosecution need only prove that it has enough evidence to take the case to trial.

The Arraignment

Assuming that the case survives the preliminary hearing (and it will), the defendant moves on to the *arraignment.*

At the arraignment, the formal charges are read to the defendant. The defendant then makes a plea of guilty, not guilty, *nolo contendere* or "who me?"

If the accused pleads guilty, he is waiving several constitutional rights – the right to a trial by jury, the right against self-incrimination, the right to confront one's accusers and even the right to wear one of those ugly orange jumpsuits every day of the trial.

Therefore, before a guilty plea is accepted, the judge will determine if the plea is voluntary. She will do so by making sure that the accused understands the nature of the charges, the possible consequences of the plea and the rights being waived.

Most guilty pleas are the result of a plea bargain. In short, the defendant agrees to plead guilty in return for a lesser punishment. This deal is made between the state and the defendant. However, the judge must also agree to the terms of the plea bargain.

The plea of *nolo contendere* means that the defendant neither admits nor denies the charges but agrees to take the punishment anyway. This is commonly referred to as pleading "no contest."

For most practical purposes, this is a guilty plea. However, one big difference is that a plea of *nolo contendere* can't be used as an admission of guilt in a later civil trial.

Therefore, let's suppose a fictional celebrity (let's call him A.J. Simpleton) pleads *nolo contendere* to the murder of his ex-wife and her new boyfriend. This plea can't be used against him in a later civil trial. However, the fact that the plaintiffs have pictures of him wearing gloves and shoes that he claims to have never owned, will be used against him.

Even still, this is better than simply pleading guilty to the crime. A guilty plea can be used as evidence in a civil trial. In this case, the victims' families would have taken his Heisman trophy without a fight.

Also, a plea of *nolo contendere* is not considered a "conviction" for some purposes. For instance, California has a "three strike" law that imposes life sentences after a third conviction for a violent crime. However, a "no contest" plea doesn't count as a strike (it's more like a foul tip).

Right to Speedy Trial

Once the government decides to bring a case, the Sixth Amendment requires it do so "speedily." Please remember that we are talking about the government here, so "speedy" means sometime before the defendant's death by natural causes.

There is no set period of time designated as "speedy" but one year is usually the maximum. If the government fails to bring the case to trial in time, then all charges are automatically dismissed, unless the de-

fendant caused the delay.

Double Jeopardy

The Fifth Amendment states that no person shall "be subject for the same offense to be twice put in jeopardy of life or limb." In other words, no person may be tried twice for the same offense. This is the concept of "double jeopardy."

However, to be accurate, double jeopardy only prevents a person from being tried twice for the same offense *by the same state.* Therefore, a defendant may be acquitted in a state court and then tried again in federal court for the same offense (e.g., the police officers involved in the Rodney King beating).

Trial By Jury

Another fundamental right of the accused is the right to a trial by jury. The size of the jury must be at least six members (or three really fat ones).

The composition of the jury should fairly represent the community. And in no event may certain possible jurors be rejected solely on account of their race. Also, it seems that jurors can't be rejected for their inability and unwillingness to follow the facts or the law, either.

Surprisingly, the Constitution doesn't require a guilty verdict to be unanimous. In a few cases, a 9-3 vote has been upheld as constitutional. However, in all cases, the defendant must be proven guilty beyond a reasonable doubt. Unless, of course, he is a member of a racial or ethnic group you don't like. In that case, he can be merely "kind of guilty."

Sentencing

Upon conviction, the court must impose a sentence. Some judges are faced with strict sentencing guidelines. Other judges have substantial discretion in meting out punishments. However, all judges are restricted by the Eighth Amendment's prohibition against *cruel and unusual punishment.*

A punishment is cruel and unusual if it is far in excess of the punishment handed down for similarly serious offenses. Also, punishment that is inappropriate for any crime is cruel and unusual punishment. For instance, forcing a serial killer to watch Magic Johnson's short-lived TV talk show, *even once,* would be cruel and unusual.

In the case of capital punishment, the courts have repeatedly ruled that the death penalty is not cruel and unusual. Nevertheless, some methods of execution are considered cruel and unusual. For instance, in 2001, the Georgia Supreme Court ruled that electrocution was unconstitutional and required all future executions to be conducted by lethal injection.

Also, opponents of the death penalty have been able to attack executions on other grounds. For instance, in 2002, the Supreme Court banned the execution of mentally retarded inmates. Other states have placed moratoriums on executions after DNA evidence has illustrated that some previously executed inmates were actually innocent.

On the other hand, some states have picked up the pace of executions. For instance, in 2000, Texas set an all-time record of 40 executions in a single year. This feat earned Governor George W. Bush the nickname of "Texecutioner."

Other states, like California and Pennsylvania, with their extensive appeals processes, are experimenting with an entirely new method of execution – death by natural causes.

Chapter in Review
Procedural Requirements

1. The Miranda Rule requires:

   a. Police to inform suspects of their rights prior to questioning

   b. Prison officials to allow inmates access to www.miranda.com

   c. Jennifer Lopez to take some acting lessons

2. Protection against unreasonable searches and seizures is provided by:

   a. The 5th Amendment

   b. The 9th Commandment

   c. The 4th Amendment

3. Double Jeopardy refers to:

   a. A second marriage

   b. The round in Jeopardy in which the questions become harder than uncut diamonds

   c. The prohibition against being tried twice for the same crime

COURTROOM LAW

MOTIONS, OBJECTIONS AND HEARSAY ...
OH MY!

COURTROOM LAW
OVERVIEW

In this section of the book, we will explore the laws of civil procedure and evidence. In other words, you will learn how to get into court and what to do when you get there.

However, as I've said before, this is not a do-it-yourself guide to the law. Therefore, even if you memorize every word of this section, I would not encourage you to file your own lawsuit any more than I would encourage you to perform your own surgery, build your own home or program your own VCR. You should leave these tasks to doctors, contractors and your children. In fact, there is an old adage that states: "Any lawyer who represents himself has a fool for a client." Unfortunately, this adage is true in almost all attorney-client contexts.

Of course, you may be asking, "So why is this stuff in the book?" There are two basic reasons. First and foremost, I needed to add some pages to this book. After all, who is going to pay $14.95 for a 32-page pamphlet? Second, this section will serve as an excellent resource for your TV viewing.

If you are like the millions of people who enjoy *The Practice*, *Law and Order*, and *Judge Wapner's Animal Court*, then you need to get a life! But until you do, wouldn't it be nice to know what the lawyers on TV mean when they say, "Objection! That's hearsay!" or "Objection, your honor! Relevance!" or "Objection! I don't have enough lines in this scene!"?

Moreover, you can use these same principles in your personal interactions. This particularly comes in handy when arguing with your spouse. Just as they are getting on a roll, you can stand up and yell, "Objection! Argumentative!" Even if your spouse eventually leaves you, taking the house, the cars, the kids and the dog, you will have peace of mind in knowing you had the last word.

Chapter 26

CHOOSING A COURT
Eanie Meanie Minie ... Whoa!

In order to bring a lawsuit, a lawyer must first determine the proper court in which to file it. In each state, there are both federal and state courts. However, not all cases may be brought in all courts.

In fact, to sustain a lawsuit in a particular court, three requirements must be satisfied:

1) The court must have *subject matter jurisdiction* over the dispute.

2) The court must have *territorial jurisdiction* over the parties.

3) The court must be geographically located in the proper district or county (*venue*).

STATE COURTS

Subject Matter Jurisdiction

As a general matter, a state court has subject matter jurisdiction over any dispute arising between its citizens. However, in each state, there are a number of specialty courts that only hear certain types of cases. For instance, you can't bring a child custody case in traffic court. This is true even if the case arises from an incident that occurred in the backseat of a car.

Also, each state has small claims courts for commercial disputes involving less than a certain dollar amount. For instance, in California, you can bring a case in small claims court if the amount in question is less than $5,000. The maximum amount in each state ranges from $15,000 in Tennessee to $3.50 in Arkansas.

One advantage of small claims court is that it allows people to resolve minor disputes without enduring lengthy delays, attorneys' fees and most importantly, jurors. In the past, if your neighbor owed you $300 for an old debt, you were out of luck. After all, just an introduction to an attorney usually costs more than $300. Besides, by the time your case wound its way through the judicial system, your great grandchildren usually lost interest in the outcome.

However, with small claims court, you may now embarrass yourself on *Judge Joe Brown* in even the most trivial dispute.

Now, assuming the proper state court is chosen, it will almost certainly have subject matter jurisdiction over the case. As a general rule, a state court has subject matter jurisdiction over *all* disputes between its citizens. This is true even if the case involves a violation of federal law.

For instance, let's suppose a business owner, Sexist Steven, institutes a new dress code, requiring the women to wear skirts shorter than the Artist *Currently* Known as Prince.

Not surprisingly, Steven is sued within the *hour* for violating federal civil rights laws, which prohibit discrimination on the basis of race, gender, religion, national origin, intelligence, work ethic, ability to show up before 11 a.m., etc. In this case, Steven can be sued in both federal and state courts.

Territorial Jurisdiction

Although state courts have virtually unlimited subject matter jurisdiction, they have more limited *territorial jurisdiction*. In general, a state court only has territorial jurisdiction over its citizens.

For instance, let's suppose Chatty Kathy takes a flight from her home state of New York to visit her sister in Texas. On the flight, she is seated next to Tired Timmy, who is traveling through Dallas on his way home to California. During the flight, Kathy talks and talks and talks until Timmy begins banging his head against the window in an effort to lose consciousness and finally get some sleep.

Upon arriving in Texas, Kathy disembarks and thinks nothing further of the matter, as it is a common occurrence for her. However, weeks later, Timmy can't get Kathy's

The Cost of Legal Advice

A man walked into a lawyer's office and inquired about the lawyer's rates. "$300.00 for three questions," replied the lawyer. "Isn't that awfully steep?" asked the man. "Yes," the lawyer replied. "Now," the lawyer continued, "what was your third question?"

voice out of his head and eventually seeks psychiatric care. Timmy then sues Kathy for intentional infliction of emotional distress, common law nuisance and just plain "talking too darn much."

If Timmy brings his lawsuit in California, Kathy can claim that the court doesn't have territorial jurisdiction over her. For a California court to have territorial jurisdiction over Kathy, she must either reside in the state or have certain *minimum contacts* with the state.

To establish minimum contacts with a state, a person must usually either own property located in the state or regularly conduct business in the state. For instance, if it's discovered that Kathy owns several "I Can't Get Her Voice Out of My Head" psychiatric centers in California, then she has minimum contacts with the state and may be sued in California.

Venue

Finally, even if Kathy has minimum contacts with the state, she may still contest territorial jurisdiction on the basis that the location of the court is inconvenient due to the location of the parties, witnesses or the evidence. This is called *forum non conveniens*, which is Latin for "I'm not going all the way out there just to get sued!"

Of course, even if Kathy successfully contests territorial jurisdiction and venue, she may still be sued by Timmy. However, in this case, Timmy would have to sue her in New York. And considering Timmy's last airplane experience, this is highly unlikely.

FEDERAL COURTS

Unlike state courts, federal courts have limited subject matter jurisdiction. In fact, federal courts only have two types of subject matter jurisdiction:

- **Diversity jurisdiction; and**

- **Federal question jurisdiction.**

Diversity Jurisdiction

Diversity jurisdiction exists when the parties are located in different states and the case involves more than the threshold amount (currently $75,000). Despite the straightforward nature of this rule, diversity jurisdiction is often more hotly contested than a debate over abortion, gay marriage or whether I should have written a book full of jokes about my wife's cooking.

Even when there is no obvious reason to try the case in federal courts, many lawyers will fight to do so anyway. For these lawyers, there is probably no greater joy than to say, "I'd love to stay and chat but I've got to run. I'm try-ing a case in *federal* court in the morning."

Federal Question Jurisdiction

In addition, a case may be brought in federal court if it involves a question of federal law. For instance, let's suppose you buy shares in InClown, a bio-tech company. Days later, the company announces that the FDA has rejected its new drug to reduce painful swelling of the feet and nose. However, just before the announcement, a well-known celebrity, Marsha Steward, sells her shares in the company ("It's a good thing!").

Days later, the SEC announces an investigation of the well-known celebrity for insider trading. If you de-

cide to bring your own private lawsuit in federal court, the court will have subject matter jurisdiction over the case. This is the case even if your claim is for only $12.95.

As for territorial jurisdiction and venue, the same principles apply in federal court as apply in state court. In order to be sued in federal court in California, a person must reside in the state, have minimum contacts with the state or just be really wealthy.

Chapter in Review
Choosing a Court

1. Which of the following is NOT necessary for diversity jurisdiction?

    a. The parties are citizens of different states

    b. The amount in question exceeds $75,000

    c. A lawsuit by the NAACP

2. A person will satisfy the "minimum contacts" test if he:

    a. Passes out business cards at the local Chamber of Commerce

    b. Conducts business in the state

    c. Marries my wife

3. Which of the following justifies *forum non coveniens?*

    a. All the evidence is located in another state

    b. Courthouse traffic is horrible

    c. What was the question again?

Chapter 27

PRE-TRIAL ACTIVITY
Landing the First Blow

THE COMPLAINT

The first salvo launched in any lawsuit is the complaint. In the complaint, the plaintiff claims that the defendant has done something wrong and, as a result, the plaintiff has suffered some harm.

If you have ever been married, then you are already familiar with complaints. However, legal complaints are different from spousal complaints in two ways.

For one, you must take legal complaints seriously. Secondly, a legal complaint must actually have some basis in logic and reality. In fact, a legal complaint must set forth facts that, if true, would entitle the plaintiff to some *legal remedy*.

Therefore, let's suppose Thoughtful Theresa and Thoughtless Theodore have been dating for several months. Although Theresa often does thoughtful things for Theodore, he never reciprocates. In fact, during the entire course of their relationship, Theodore has never once called just to see how Theresa was doing.

Although Theresa has legitimate grounds for complaint, she can't sue Theodore in federal court for being a bad boyfriend. After all, men are not legally obligated to be thoughtful, or even logical for that matter (Thank Heaven!).

Interestingly, in many states, the complaint need not state a *prayer for relief*. A prayer for relief is a request for an injunction, monetary damages or other legal remedy. Moreover, even if the plaintiff states a prayer of relief, this prayer need not be specific. For instance, it is common for plaintiffs to request "compensatory and punitive damages in an amount to be determined at trial." This is lawyerspeak for "I haven't finished putting all the zeroes at the end of this number yet."

Finally, many courts have their own local rules

The Lawyer's Prayer

Our Father, who shall be termed party of the first part,
Whose place of business is in Heaven,
Hallowed be Thy Name.

Thy Kingdom, pursuant to terms and conditions, come.
Thy will, duly uncontested, be done on earth,
In so far as existing statutes permit, as it is in Heaven.

Give us this day our daily bread, and forgive us our debts,
Notwithstanding claims, liens and legal costs, as we,
Who shall be termed party of the second part,
Forgive our debtors.

And lead us not into temptation,
But deliver us from evil,
The nature of which shall be determined by the Court.
For Thine is the Kingdom and the Power
And, pending appeal, the Glory forever.

Amen

regarding the complaint. For instance, some courts require that filings be written on certain-sized paper, that pages be clipped and not stapled or vice versa, that bribes be delivered in person as opposed to in the mail, etc.

NOTE FROM THE AUTHOR: Yes, I am kidding! Contrary to popular belief, judges do not accept bribes. Unless, of course, they are properly stapled to the complaint in accordance with local rules.

SERVICE OF PROCESS

After filing the complaint, the plaintiff must give the defendant notice of the lawsuit against him. This notice must contain basic information about the case, such as time and place of the hearing and the nature of the lawsuit. Until the defendant receives notice, the case can't go forward.

As a result, some defendants avoid process servers as if they are carriers of communicable diseases (which they usually are). However, unless state law requires otherwise, the defendant need not be served in person. As a general rule, the plaintiff is only required to provide the best notice practicable under the circumstances.

For instance, let's suppose Elusive Elroy has heard rumors that he is being sued for his involvement in an auto accident. To avoid service of process, Elroy stops answering his front door and begins entering and exiting his house via tunnel.

However, even these drastic measures may not be enough to prevent him from being served. For instance, in a state that allows *substitute service*, Elroy may be served by notice left with a co-worker, spouse or roommate. Also,

in a state that allows for *constructive service*, process may be served by registered mail to Elroy's last known address, publication of notice in a local newspaper, or notification of my mother-in-law, who will gladly spread the word until everyone in town knows all about the case.

THE ANSWER

Once served with the complaint, the defendant must answer the complaint within the time allowed. In the answer, the defendant may admit or deny specific allegations, raise affirmative defenses or bring counterclaims and cross-claims.

Like the complaint, the answer is made under the penalty of perjury. Nevertheless, the defendant can deny allegations in an inconsistent manner. For instance, if your neighbor sues you claiming that your dog bit him, you can answer his complaint by claiming:

(1) your dog did not bite him,

(2) your neighbor deserved to be bitten anyway, *and*

(3) it all depends on what the meaning of the word "dog" is.

Also, if the defendant has a counterclaim against the plaintiff, then he may address it in his answer. In fact, if the counterclaim arises from the circumstances in the complaint, then the defendant *must* counterclaim in his answer or never.

For instance, let's suppose you and your best friend are playing a game of "hot hands." Hot hands is a game where future ex-friends take turns trying to slap each other's hands *really* hard. As is often the case, this particular game of hot hands slowly transforms into a game of hot *face*.

Let's further suppose that, after being released from the hospital, your former best friend files a lawsuit against you for battery. If you fail to counterclaim in your answer, then you can't sue him for your injuries in the game.

Also, as a defendant, you may file cross-claims against co-defendants in your answer. For instance, if your game of "hot hands" involved another former

friend and the two of you are sued, then you may cross-claim against him as well as the plaintiff.

Lastly, in many cases, the plaintiff fails to sue everyone involved in the matter. In this case, the defendant may request that a third party be made a part of the lawsuit. For instance, let's suppose Wealthy Walter lends his car to Poor Paul. If Paul gets into an accident, the plaintiff may choose to name only Walter as a de- fendant because the chances of recovering from Paul are lower than World- Com's stock price. As a result, in his answer, Walter may request that Paul be added as a co-defendant.

CLASS ACTIONS

In some cases, a group of people will have similar claims against a defendant. In that case, they may seek to bring their cases collectively as a *class action*. In a class action, one or more people will bring a lawsuit "on behalf of all individuals similarly situated."

However, before the class action may proceed, the court must first certify the class. The court will only certify the class if it is so numerous that not all members can be reasonably named in the complaint. Therefore, Larry, Curly and Shemp could not have filed a class action against Moe for battery because it would be easy to name each of them as plaintiffs in the lawsuit. However, the millions of kids who nearly poked out each other's eyes emulating Moe could have brought a class action lawsuit against him.

In fact, in many class actions, the class is so numerous that many of the plaintiffs are unknown, even to their lawyers. For instance, in a landmark case against the tobacco companies, the plaintiffs were a class of approximately 500,000 unidentified sick smokers in Florida.

Nevertheless, the court will only certify the class if all members of the class have a common claim against the defendant. For instance, in the Florida tobacco case, all of the plaintiffs had something in common – they were idiots. Seriously, in this case, all class members claimed that tobacco either had made them sick or will make them sick in the future. Therefore, the court certified their class action.

However, a court would not certify a class of the millions of people who are bothered by Dennis Rodman. This is because Dennis is bothersome in so many different ways. In this case, the classes would have to be split into groups: those who are bothered by his tattoos and nose-rings; those who are bothered by his on-court antics; those who are bothered by his off-court antics; those who think he looks hideous in a wedding gown; etc.

NOTE FROM THE PUBLISHER: Notwithstanding the author, we are big fans of Dennis Rodman at Lawpsided Press. In fact, we would like to invite him to a tour of our facilities, provided he adheres to our "No Shirt, No Pants, No Service" policy.

A *Lawpsided* View
Class Actions

In 2001, Wal-Mart endured the wrath of more than 700,000 women in the nation's largest sex discrimination lawsuit not involving Bill Clinton. Six women brought the lawsuit on behalf of all former and current female employees of Wal-Mart, claiming that the retailer discriminated against women in hiring, promotions and pay.

As a graduate of our public school system, it may be difficult to truly grasp the magnitude of a large number like 700,000 (or even read your own name). Therefore, think of it this way ... A trip of 700,000 miles is the equivalent of circling the globe 28 times (or enduring one of my father's infamous cross-country car trips).

In their complaint, the women claimed that they hit the proverbial "glass ceiling" and were later terminated or demoted when they complained to their superiors. Furthermore, they claimed that only men were placed in "high profile" departments, such as furniture, hardware, electronics, guns, chewing tobacco, etc. They also claimed that, when given jobs in these male-dominated areas, they were subjected to a hostile work environment.

For instance, one plaintiff claims that she was regularly called the "B-word" by her male supervisors during her tenure in the Tire Mounting Department. On one occasion, she reports entering the waiting area only to find her co-workers watching porn.

As a responsible journalist, I called Wal-Mart representatives to confirm these allegations. The answers I received were troubling, to say the least. For one, that store is not currently hiring for positions in the Tire Mounting Department. Moreover, they can't guarantee that porn will be shown at *all times* in the waiting room.

Another common complaint is that Wal-Mart requires constant relocations for those on the "career track." The plaintiffs claim that these relocations are unnecessary and only serve to prevent women from competing for these positions. For instance, one plaintiff was relocated ten times over four states in just a few years.

These constant relocations seem quite burdensome to me. I couldn't imagine saying, "Hey, baby! That big promotion finally came through. You are now looking at the Assistant to the Assistant Shift Supervisor in Hosiery. Pack your bags and get the kids out of school. We're off to Fresno!"

Nevertheless, if the plaintiffs are successful in certifying a class size of 700,000 plaintiffs, even the slightest discrimination on the part of Wal-Mart could be costly. For instance, if a jury imposes damages of just $1,000 per employee, the total award would be $700 million. It is not hard to see how the damages in this case could run into the billions. A billion dollar verdict in this case will not bankrupt Wal-Mart but it may cause a major shake-up in executive management. This means that there may be a position opening up in the Tire Mounting department after all.

DISCOVERY

After the parties have exchanged complaints and answers, the discovery phase of the case begins. Interestingly, you are not required to know all of the facts *before* filing a lawsuit. In fact, you can be as clueless as a supermodel at a nuclear physics convention, just so long as you have a good faith belief that the allegations in your complaint are true. Then, during the discovery phase of the case, you will be given the opportunity to discover the true facts.

Please note that the procedural rules regarding discovery are more intricate than neurosurgery, and often, far more bloody. Therefore, the following is a very *general* overview of the discovery process.

Depositions

One method of discovery is to *depose* potential witnesses. In a deposition, the witness (the deponent) is asked questions under oath. A court reporter records the deposition and then prepares a transcript of the deposition up until the point at which he fell asleep.

Interestingly, not only may your lawyer depose the opposing party, but she may depose third parties as well. So long as a person

possesses relevant information, he may be served with a *subpoena* and then deposed.

Document Production

Your lawyer may also obtain information by requesting the other party to produce documents for your inspection. In this request, your lawyer must include a list of documents to be produced and a time and location for inspection.

Interrogatories

Your lawyer may also serve written *interrogatories* on the other party. An interrogatory is a request for written information. However, unlike depositions, interrogatories may be requested only from parties to the lawsuit.

When responding to interrogatories, you must provide all requested information that is known to you. You must also provide all information that, although not known, is discoverable through reasonable inspection.

For instance, let's suppose you receive a written interrogatory requesting your wife's date of birth. Let's further suppose that you haven't memorized this information (although you have memorized the lifetime batting average of every major league baseball player since 1889). In this case, you would be compelled to provide her date of birth even if you had to sneak into her purse while she's asleep and copy the information from her driver's license.

A Sample Interrogatory

In order to prevent opposing counsel from objecting to an interrogatory on the grounds that it is unclear or confusing, a lawyer will go to great lengths to make it as clear as possible. Unfortunately, this practice of painstaking questioning sometimes seeps over into other aspects of the lawyer's life. Here is how I ask my children if they've cleaned their rooms:

"Did you, in any manner whatsoever, physically arrange, straighten, order, classify or sort any of the items contained in, or around, the immediate vicinity of the room in which you primarily sleep, slumber or otherwise rest, and which contains the vast majority of your personal property and chattel, including but not limited to, your clothes, video games, computer equipment and other personal effects and belongings, in such a manner so that the aforementioned area would be considered "clean" in accordance with Sections 2-6 and 12 of the House Rules (a copy of which is displayed on the refrigerator)?"

Sanctions

Often disputes arise during the discovery process. One party will deny a discovery request claiming that it is irrelevant, protected by privilege or just plain stupid. In this case, the judge must determine whether the request should be permitted.

If the judge rules in favor of the requesting party, then the other party must respond to the request. If the party still refuses, then he is subject to a number of sanctions.

For one, the judge can hold him in contempt of court and throw him in jail indefinitely. Also, the judge can require him to pay the other party's legal fees and costs in the matter.

More importantly, ignoring a court order can prejudice your case more severely than Archie Bunker serving as foreman on the O.J. Simpson jury.

For instance, let's suppose Hacking Harry is being sued for industrial espionage for breaking into a competitor's computer system. In his answer, Harry claims that the allegations are impossible because he knows nothing about computers. However, the plaintiff believes that Harry has a doctorate in computer science from M.I.T. and gets the judge to order Harry to turn over his college transcripts.

If Harry refuses, then the judge may prevent Harry from claiming computer illiteracy at trial. Moreover, the judge can impose a more serious sanction – he can force Harry to eat at the M.I.T. cafeteria. Finally, the judge can impose the ultimate sanction by simply entering a judgment in favor of the plaintiff.

Chapter in Review
Pre-Trial Activity

1. Which comes first?
    a. The complaint
    b. The answer
    c. The second job to pay your legal fees

2. A class of plaintiffs will be certified if:
    a. They pass the written exam
    b. They pass the oral exam
    c. They are numerous and have a common complaint

3. Where can a deposition be taken?
    a. Only in a bus depot
    b. Only in a courtroom
    c. Anywhere, so long as a court reporter is present

AT TRIAL
"Let's Get It On!"

Often, during the discovery process, the parties will learn something useful to help them better evaluate their cases. As a result, cases are usually settled prior to trial. However, in some instances, the parties can see no more eye-to-eye than Shaquille O'Neal and Mary Lou Retton. In this situation, the case goes to trial.

There are two types of trials:

- **Bench trials**
- **Jury trials**

In a bench trial, the judge (or a panel of judges) hears the evidence and then makes a ruling. In a jury trial, the judge runs the trial and determines the evidence that may be admitted but the jury decides the outcome of the case.

JURY SELECTION

In jury trials, the lawyers must first select a jury. Generally, a pool of potential jurors is selected for questioning, or *voir dire.*

During this process, each lawyer is allowed to question prospective jurors to determine if they can render a fair and impartial verdict.

These questions usually delve into whether the juror has a relationship with a party in the case, a financial interest in the case, the "hots" for one of the lawyers, etc. If *voir dire* reveals a juror's bias, then either party may challenge that juror's inclusion on the jury for cause.

Many states also allow jurors to be challenged *peremptorily.* In other words, a lawyer can have a juror removed from the panel for any reason, or none at all. However, each lawyer only has a limited number of peremptory challenges. On the other hand, there is no limit to the number of challenges for cause.

OPENING STATEMENTS

Now, assuming that *voir dire* takes no longer than it took to build an Egyptian

pyramid, the trial is ready to begin. The first stage of the trial is opening statements, which will certainly take longer than building a pyramid.

During opening statements, each lawyer gives the jury a preview of her case. Although opening statements receive considerable attention from the media, they have no real impact on the outcome of the case, much like the truth, itself.

EVIDENCE

Once opening statements are complete, then the "real" trial begins, as each side presents its evidence.

The rules of evidence are complex and vary from state to state. However, on the following pages, you will learn some of the basic principles of evidence to use while watching L.A. Law re-runs on cable television.

Relevance

The main thrust of the rules of evidence is to ensure that only relevant evidence is admitted at trial. Relevant evidence is evidence with *probative value*. Or, in other words, relevant evidence tends to prove a fact that is important to the outcome of the case.

Relevant evidence comes in two forms:

- **Direct**

- **Circumstantial**

Direct evidence proves the fact while circumstantial evidence simply infers it. For instance, this book *proves* that I am in serious need of psychiatric care. Likewise, it *infers* that my wife is equally insane for putting up with me. However, this book doesn't prove that my wife is insane because it's possible that she hasn't read it. In fact, considering all the jokes about her cooking, I can assure you that she hasn't read it.

To better illustrate this distinction, let's suppose that a witness testifies that she saw an alien spacecraft land and abduct her husband. This is direct evidence of an alien abduction. As you can see, direct evidence is not necessarily true.

On the other hand, let's suppose this same witness testifies that her husband came home at 3 a.m. with marks on his arms and back. This is only circumstantial evidence of an alien abduction since there are other possible explanations for his "disappearance" – Donna, Linda, Debbie, etc.

As a general rule, all relevant evidence is admissible at trial. Of course, as you will see, there are several exceptions to this rule. And even worse, there are exceptions to the exceptions.

Witnesses

One method of introducing evidence is to call witnesses to testify at trial. As a general matter, any person who can communicate clearly and comprehend the duty to tell the truth may testify in court.

Moreover, even if a witness suffers from a communication disability, such as being deaf, mute or a professional boxer, he may still testify through the use of an interpreter. For the most part, only judges, jurors and people covered by a privilege are barred from testifying in the case.

Privileges

To foster communication in some relationships, the law shields those communications from being introduced into evidence. The rationale is that people should feel secure enough in these relationships to reveal confidences without the threat of going to prison or being sued. The following is a list of these privileged relationships:

- **Husband-wife**
- **Attorney-client**
- **Therapist-patient**
- **Clergy-penitent**

As a result of the marital privilege, you can't be forced to testify against your spouse in a criminal action. However, in many states, you can be compelled to testify against your spouse in a civil action.

Of course, there are several limitations to the privilege. For one, although your spouse can't be compelled to testify against you, he can choose to do so in some states. And if the lawsuit involves a dispute between the couple, such as a divorce, then the privilege doesn't apply at all. And finally, the privilege only exists so long as you are married. If you get divorced, your former spouse will be free (and probably *extremely* willing) to testify against you.

In the attorney-client relationship, the attorney may not reveal any confidences told to her while rendering legal services for the client. Unlike the marriage privilege, this privilege continues after the attorney-client relationship ends.

This privilege protects communications about *past* crimes in order to allow the attorney to effectively represent her client. However, the privilege does not prevent a lawyer from warning others about *future* crimes.

This same philosophy applies to the therapist-patient and clergy-penitent privileges. Therefore, if you confess past crimes to your therapist or priest, then he may not disclose those crimes to the authorities. However, if you discuss plans for future crimes with him, then he may reveal your confidences. In fact, in some cases, he *must* warn others about your plans.

Direct Examination

At trial, each party is allowed to call witnesses to testify on its behalf. This is called *direct examination.* During direct examination, the lawyer is normally prevented from asking leading questions. After all, sympathetic witnesses are often susceptible to the lawyer's suggestions.

Lawyer: "So you were in your backyard chipping golf balls when you realized that you were late for your flight, so you dashed through your house, like in a Hertz commercial, getting sweaty and cutting your finger in the process, right?"

Witness: "Yeah, whatever he just said!"

Obviously, the witness is supposed to tell his story in his own words (carefully crafted beforehand by his lawyer, of course). Therefore, leading questions are not usually allowed in direct examination.

However, leading questions are allowed when the witness is giving preliminary information, such as name, address, occupation, etc. Also, leading questions are allowed when the witness has the mental capacity of a child or an accountant at Arthur Andersen.

Cross Examination

However, leading questions are allowed on cross examination, where the witness is usually hostile.

Also, a witness' credibility (or lack thereof) is an important consideration for the jury. Therefore, on cross examination, the lawyer is allowed to test the witness' credibility. This is usually done by trying to prove that the witness was either lying or mistaken about his testimony.

For instance, let's suppose Myopic Michael is an eyewitness for the plaintiff in a case. Michael testifies that, while at the window of his 45th story apartment, he saw the defendant spit on the plaintiff. On cross

examination, the defendant's lawyer will try to demonstrate that Michael could not possibly have seen the incident clearly from so far away.

Lawyer: "Michael, is it your testimony that you saw my client spit on the plaintiff from a distance of over 300 feet away?"

Witness: "Yes."

Lawyer: "I see that you wear eyeglasses, sir. Can you tell us your eyesight without glasses?"

Witness: "20/600"

Lawyer: "Whoa! Did they give you a seeing-eye dog with those glasses? Or does the dog come separately?"

Witness: "No! And, with my eyeglasses on, I can see perfectly fine."

Lawyer: "By the thickness of the lenses, I'd guess you can see all the way into the future. By the way, did you have them on when you *imagined* seeing my client spitting on the plaintiff?"

Witness: "Well, not exactly."

Lawyer: "So let me see if I understand this ... you expect this court to believe that you could see a man spitting from 300 feet away despite the fact that if we took your glasses away from you now, you wouldn't be able to find your way off the stand?"

In truth, the preceding exchange more resembles something that you'd see on a television show. In real life, the plaintiff's lawyer would have interrupted the questioning on several occasions with objections.

For one, a lawyer may not ask the witness compound questions. In this case, the lawyer asked a compound question in reference to the seeing-eye dog. As a result, the witness' answer of "no" is unclear. If he was answering the first question, then he was denying that a seeing-eye dog came with his glasses. However, if he was answering the second question, then he was affirming that a seeing-eye dog was included with his glasses. As you can see, compound questions can lead to confusion for the jurors, who, in most cases, are already confused enough.

Second, a lawyer may not ask a question that is misleading or assumes a fact not in evidence. For instance, the lawyer asks, "did you have [the eye-glasses] on when you *imagined* seeing my client spit on the plaintiff?" This question assumes that the witness imagined the event.

If the witness were forced to answer this question, then, regardless of the answer, the jury might assume that the entire incident was a figment of his imagination.

Third, a lawyer may not use questions to make arguments to the jury. Of course, this is not to say that the lawyer should not have a point to his questions. However, he should simply present the evidence to the jury and let the jury come to its own conclusions. For instance, in our example, the last question is simply an argument that the witness' eyewitness testimony is unreliable. However, this is a conclusion

---

The World's Worst Cross Examiner

Lawyer: "Doctor, is it possible that the patient was alive when you began the autopsy?"

Witness: "No."

Lawyer: "How can you be so sure, Doctor?"

Witness: "Because his brain was sitting on my desk in a jar."

Lawyer: "But could the patient have still been alive nevertheless?"

Doctor: "Sure. It is possible that he could have been alive and practicing law somewhere."

for the jury to formulate on its own (with a little help from the lawyers during closing arguments).

Character Evidence

Evidence of a witness' character is relevant evidence and therefore, admissible because it has probative value. However, in some situations, it may be more prejudicial than probative. As a result, character evidence is not usually allowed for the purpose of proving the person committed some act.

This is particularly true in criminal trials. Therefore, even if the defendant has a rap sheet longer than Dom Deluise's shopping list, the prosecution can't introduce evidence of prior convictions.

For instance, let's suppose Thieving Theodore is on trial for shoplifting. Theodore was arrested after fitting the store clerk's description of the assailant. Let's further suppose that Theodore has been caught shoplifting more often than Winona Ryder. As a general rule, the prosecution can't introduce evidence of his prior convictions to prove he is guilty of shoplifting in this case.

However, as always, there are several exceptions to this rule. One exception is when the prior bad acts show a pattern that helps identify the offender. For instance, let's suppose Theodore has a history of shoplifting while wearing nothing more than chaps and a bandana. The prosecution can introduce this evidence if the shoplifter in this case was similarly dressed.

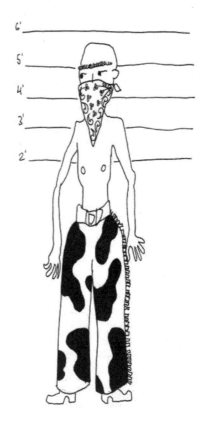

Another exception to this rule is when the prior bad acts are introduced in order to impeach the defendant's claims of good moral character. For instance, let's suppose Battering Bobby is on trial for assault and battery. In his testimony, Bobby says, "I would never do such a thing. I wouldn't hurt a fly." As a result, during cross examination, the prosecution can ask Bobby about his 347 other battery convictions.

Also, please note that although character evidence is often inadmissible, evidence of habit or routine is usually admissible. For instance, let's take the case of Sticky Steven, who is so named because of his penchant for theft and his love of peanut butter. If Steven is on trial for embezzlement, then evidence of his prior crimes is probably not admissible. However, the prosecution can introduce evidence of his love of peanut butter, particularly if the embezzler left behind a trail of *Jif*.

Hearsay

As discussed earlier, cross examination is crucial in accessing a witness' credibility. As a result, except in *extremely* rare cases, opposing counsel must be given the opportu-

nity to cross examine each witness.

To this end, the courts have developed the *hearsay rule.* Unfortunately, this rule is more difficult to comprehend than the success of The Backstreet Boys. After reading this section, if you have any understanding of this rule at all, you will be ahead of 90% of the practicing lawyers in America (including me). However, it's important to discuss hearsay because although you will never use it yourself, you will hear this term repeatedly on *The Practice.*

In short, the hearsay rule prevents a witness from testifying as to what someone else said. For instance, let's suppose my wife witnesses my 6-year-old son putting quarters into the floppy drive of my computer *again.* Finally realizing that repeated warnings and timeouts have been ineffective, I resort to more drastic measures – I sue him.

However, because of the hearsay rule, I can't testify at trial as to what my wife saw. If I am to prevail in court, I must convince my

wife to testify against "her baby."

The reason for the hearsay rule is because hearsay evidence doesn't provide an adequate opportunity for cross examination. As we've discussed, opposing counsel uses cross examination to test the credibility of the witness. However, if the witness is relying on the report of a third party, there is no way for opposing counsel to test the third party's credibility.

That being said, it is important to clarify that the hearsay rule doesn't apply to *all* third party statements. The hearsay rule only bars third party statements introduced as assertions of fact.

NOTE FROM THE AUTHOR: If you now have a headache, then please take two aspirin before reading further because, trust me, things are going to get much worse before they get better.

NOTE FROM THE PUBLISHER: Lawpsided Press hereby disclaims all liability for any migraines, ulcers or acts of spontaneous combustion that result from trying to understand the hearsay rule. By reading further, you *assume the risk.*

For instance, let's suppose your best friend invites you over to watch the latest pay-per-view boxing match promoted by Don King. As usual, the fight ends in the first round, leaving your friend feeling frustrated and cheated. In

a fit of anger, he says, "Don King is a swindler and a cheat!"

Let's further suppose that you are called as a witness at Don King's next fraud trial. In this case, you can't repeat your best friend's comment for the purpose of proving that Don King is a fraud. This would be an example of inadmissible hearsay evidence.

On the other hand, let's suppose that instead you are called as a witness in Don King's slander suit against your best friend. In this case, your best friend's statement is admissible because it won't be introduced to prove Mr. King is a fraud (we already know that). Instead, his statement will be introduced merely to prove that the slanderous statement was made.

Also, the hearsay rule doesn't apply in the case where a person confesses his wrongdoing. For instance, let's suppose Freddy the Financier gets drunk at a party and announces that he has just committed several acts of securities fraud. In this case, any witness to this statement can repeat it at trial to prove that Freddy is guilty of securities fraud.

In addition, hearsay evidence may be introduced to

impeach the credibility of a witness. If the witness has made statements that are inconsistent with his current testimony, then those prior statements may be introduced to impeach his credibility.

For instance, let's suppose Contractor Carl works in the construction trade in New York City. During happy hours, Carl often tells his friends of kickbacks and shakedowns that occur at his company.

If Carl is called to testify against his boss, Sammy "The Unicorn" Graciano, then he will likely deny any knowledge of wrongdoing (or of his own name, for that matter). However, the prosecution may present contradictory hearsay evidence from Carl's friends, provided that one of them is crazy enough to testify against a man nicknamed "The Unicorn."

Documentary Evidence

A second method for introducing evidence is to present documents to the jury. Any relevant document may be admitted into evidence so long as it has been *authenticated*. In

other words, the document must be legitimate.

A document may be authenticated in a number of ways. In some cases, a lawyer will call the author of the document to testify that she wrote it. In other cases, a signer or witness to the document may be called for authentication.

In some cases, a person familiar with a signature on the document will be called to testify. Likewise, a handwriting expert may be used for authentication purposes. However, more often than not, the parties will simply *stipulate* (agree) that the document is accurate.

When the contents of the document are important to the case, then courts look to the *best evidence rule*. Historically, this rule required the parties to produce original documents.

Until fairly recently, copies of documents were produced by hand. As a result, the risk of error was higher than Al Sharpton's cholesterol count. Therefore, parties were often required to sign several sets of documents to ensure that an original document would be available in case of a dispute.

However, this was before the days of copying machines, scanners and fat-free potato chips. In the 21st century, copies and even faxes can be introduced into evidence. Nevertheless, this seems to have escaped the notice of mortgage companies, which insist that you sign a stack of documents higher than Mount Everest, only far more time-consuming to tackle.

Demonstrative Evidence

As the name implies, demonstrative evidence is tangible evidence used to explain or demonstrate a point. Photographs, x-rays and charts are examples of demonstrative evidence.

Like documentary evidence, demonstrative evidence must be authenticated. Also, the party introducing this evidence must establish a chain of custody that demonstrates that the evidence has not been altered or tampered with.

In most cases, demonstrative evidence is presented alongside witness testimony. As a result, the witness usually authenticates that the picture, model or other illustrative tool accurately represents the real thing.

Scientific Evidence

Scientific evidence is evidence derived from technological or scientific methods. Examples are blood tests, DNA matches, ballistic tests, etc. To present this evidence, you must have a sound scientific foundation that is generally accepted as reliable within the scientific community.

To establish a scientific foundation, you must show that the test was performed in a generally accepted manner. For instance, a party may not introduce DNA evidence based upon results derived from a high school chemistry set.

Likewise, to use the evidence produced by radar guns and breathalyzers, law enforcement officers must demonstrate that the equipment was used properly and maintained in good condition.

Finally, scientific evidence must be regarded as reliable by members of the scientific community. As a result, polygraphs and hypnosis are no more admissible than Ouija boards and testimony from Mark Fuhrman.

Opinion

As we've discussed earlier, the jury is responsible for drawing conclusions from the evidence. As a result, witnesses are not usually permitted to give their opinions. Or, in the immortal words of Joe Friday from Dragnet, "Just the facts, ma'am."

For instance, let's suppose Dumb Donald brings a lawsuit against the publisher of The Guinness Book of World Records. In his lawsuit, he claims that he should have been named the "Dumbest Person in the World." Donald asks you to testify in court as to his stupidity.

At trial, you can tell the jurors about the many instances in which Donald exhibited the intelligence of a pork chop. However, you can't give your opinion of his general level of intelligence unless you are an expert on such matters (e.g., you are a doctor, psychologist or Dan Quayle's best friend).

Experts are allowed to give their professional opinions about any relevant aspect of a case. In some types of cases, expert testimony is almost required. For instance, in legal malpractice cases, each party will present an expert witness to testify why the defendant's conduct was, or was not, malpractice.

Of course, experts must be qualified to give their opinions based upon scientific, technical or other training. Therefore, even if you watched every minute of the O.J. trial on TV, you are not qualified to give expert testimony in court. Unless, of course, you testify as an expert of people who have entirely too much free time on their hands.

Judicial Notice

Although most facts in a case must be introduced by producing witnesses, documentary evidence and the like, the court will take *judicial notice* of generally known facts. For instance, it isn't necessary to introduce testimony from a geologist to prove that the sun sets in the west. The court will take judicial notice of this fact.

In civil trials, if the court takes judicial notice of a fact, then the jury must accept it as truth. However, in criminal trials, the jury may disregard this fact, as well as the law, logic or reality.

CLOSING ARGUMENTS

After each party has presented its evidence, the lawyers will be allowed to make closing arguments. In these arguments, the lawyers will attempt to tie together the various pieces of evidence so that 12 people with a combined I.Q. of 13 can make the "right" decision.

Chapter in Review
At Trial

1. What is *voir dire?*
   a. A $65.00 appetizer at a fancy French restaurant
   b. The process by which lawyers question prospective jurors
   c. Two or more deer

2. When does the marital privilege no longer apply?
   a. Immediately after the honey-moon
   b. After your first child is born
   c. Upon divorce

3. The purpose of the hearsay rule is to:
   a. Prevent witnesses from giving testimony that is not subject to cross examination
   b. Give law students nightmares
   c. Make your head hurt
   d. All of the above

Chapter 20

REACHING A DECISION
"And the Winner is ..."

After each side has presented its evidence, it's usually time for the case to go to the jury. However, in some cases, the lawyers may seek to prevent a jury verdict.

TRIAL MOTIONS

Motion for Non-Suit

At the end of the plaintiff's case, the defendant may bring a *motion for non-suit*. In this motion, the defendant argues that the plaintiff hasn't presented any substantial evidence to support its case and as a result, the case should be dismissed.

Courts are reluctant to grant motions for non-suit. Judges aren't usually inclined to substitute their judgment for the jury's. Therefore, unless the plaintiff's case is weaker than ABC's fall line-up, the judge will not grant a motion for non-suit.

Motion for Directed Verdict

After both sides have presented their evidence, either party may move for a directed verdict. Much like a motion for non-suit, a directed verdict will only be granted when the case couldn't be more open and shut if the judge's mother-in-law's fingers were wedged in the courthouse doors.

JURY INSTRUCTIONS

If the case survives a motion for non-suit or a motion for directed verdict, then the judge will deliver instructions to the jury. In her instructions, the judge will discuss the burden of proof and the legal standard to be applied in the case.

Burden of Proof

In a civil trial, the plaintiff has the burden of producing evidence to support her theory of the case. In most cases, the plaintiff will have to prove her case by a *preponderance of the evidence.* Or, in other words, the plaintiff must convince the jury that her version of the facts is more likely true than the defendant's version.

Likewise, in a criminal trial, the prosecution has the burden of producing evidence to support its case. However, unlike in a civil case, in a criminal trial, the prosecution must prove its case *beyond a reasonable doubt.*

This standard requires the jury to be convinced to a "moral certainty." This does not mean that the jury must be 100% certain that the defendant is guilty. After all, this level of certainty is only attainable when dealing with so-called "black and white" subjects, such as mathematics, the laws of physics or Tiger Woods' continued domination of the PGA Tour.

Therefore, "beyond a reasonable doubt" does not mean beyond *any* doubt. It simply means that the jury is convinced beyond any real or measurable doubt that the defendant committed the crime.

Interestingly, in some situations, the burden of proof switches to the defendant. This occurs when the defendant has committed the act but has some af-

firmative defense under the law.

To illustrate this point, let's use an *extremely* hypothetical example. Let's suppose that certain celebrities and politicians are offended by the comments made about them in a certain legal humor book. Let's further suppose they sue the witty and oh-so-handsome author for libel.

In this case, proving the plaintiffs' case will be easier than Monica Lewinsky. However, the author will counter that he has a defense to libel – the truth. If the author's statements about the plaintiffs are true, then he is not liable for libel. However, in this case, the author has the burden of proving the truth of his statements. This will also be much easier than Monika Lewinsky.

NOTE FROM THE PUBLISHER: We would like to point out that none of the statements in this book is defamatory. These statements are simply jokes made in good fun and demonstrate no intent to defame anyone on the part of the publisher, the author or their respective offshore holding companies, which are, incidentally, exempt from all U.S. tort liability.

Legal Standards

In her jury instructions, the judge will clearly define the elements of the crime or the civil action. For instance, in a criminal trial for assault, the jury may be instructed to find the defendant guilty of assault *only* if the evidence shows beyond a reasonable doubt that the defendant touched or struck the victim in a manner that was offensive or harmful. Also, if the defendant has raised a defense during trial, then the judge will instruct the jury as to the availability of that defense.

OVERTURNING THE VERDICT

Judgment N.O.V.

After receiving instructions, the jury retires to deliberate. After weeks, days or just minutes, the jury returns with a verdict. After the verdict has been handed down, the losing party may then ask for a judgment notwithstanding the verdict, or *judgment*

n.o.v. In essence, in this motion, the losing party argues that no jury in its right mind could have ruled for the other party and therefore, the judge should exercise his good sense and overturn the verdict.

Understandably, judges are reluctant to grant this type of motion. In many cases, the judge has previously denied a motion for directed verdict. By granting a *judgment n.o.v.*, she would be admitting to being wrong the first time.

Secondly, some judges are elected by the voters, some of whom actually serve on juries. Therefore, these judges hesitate to overrule their constituents.

Nevertheless, judges do grant motions for *judgment n.o.v.* on occasion. For instance, in the famous British au pair case, the judge overturned the jury's second degree murder conviction and substituted a manslaughter charge.

Appeals

As a last ditch effort, the losing party may appeal the decision to a higher court. As a general matter, appellate courts only review the trial court's actions for *legal* errors.

In other words, the appeals court won't usually re-evaluate the evidence and replace the jury's judgment with its own. However, it will examine whether the trial judge admitted the proper evidence or gave proper instructions to the jury.

However, even if the appeals court finds a legal error, it will not necessarily overturn the verdict. In most cases, it will apply what is called the "harmless error" standard. In other words, unless the error likely would have resulted in a different outcome, then the appeals court will not order a new trial.

Chapter in Review
Reaching a Decision

1. To grant a motion for directed verdict, the judge must find:

   a. God

   b. $20,000 in an unmarked envelope

   c. That a reasonable jury could not have ruled for the other party

2. In a civil trial, the plaintiff must prove his case by:

   a. A nose

   b. A preponderance of the evidence

   c. Any means necessary

3. Which of the following is NOT "harmless error"?

   a. The judge mispronounces the name of the bailiff

   b. The judge's last name is Ito

   c. The judge constantly refers to the defendant as "Mr. Guilty"

Index

Index

Index

ABOUT THE AUTHOR

 Sean Carter is a lawyer, stand-up comedian, humor writer, public speaker and author. His weekly humor column appears in newspapers across the country. In addition, he is the legal commentary for a number of national magazines and web sites.

Mr. Carter is a graduate of Harvard Law School. He began his legal career as a corporate lawyer serving such clients as GNC, J. Crew, Safelite Auto Glass, The Boston Beer Company, Homeside Lending and Experian. Most recently, he was the General Counsel of NC Capital Corporation, a leading supplier of mortgage products to Wall Street.

As a stand-up comedian, Mr. Carter has appeared at venues across the country and has been a regular at the world famous Improv. As a public speaker, Mr. Carter attempts to blend humor, motivation and practical legal knowledge to entertain, inform and inspire his audiences.

Mr. Carter lives in southern California with his wife, Renee, and two sons, Austin and Matthew.

To book Mr. Carter for your next corporate event, write or fax to him in care of Lawpsided Press or e-mail him at sean@lawpsided.com.

ABOUT THE ILLUSTRATOR

Sharon Stockdale is an award-winning fine artist and internationally recognized for her work as a graphic designer. To contact Ms. Stockdale, write or fax to her in care of Lawpsided Press or by e-mail at sharon@lawpsided.com.

Lawpsided Press
P.O. Box 1867, Chino Hills, CA 91709
Phone: (909) 393-1884, Fax: (909) 393-0922

If It Does Not Fit, Must You Acquit?

Your Humorous Guide to the Law

Did you learn something about the law? Did you have a good time doing so? Do you have friends, colleagues, clients, students or family members who would also enjoy this book? If so, please feel free to order additional copies of the book:

Quantity	Price per Book
1	$14.95
2	$12.95
3	$11.95
4-6	$10.95
7-10	$9.95
11+	*Call us for prices*

Number of Books	_____
x Price per Book	_____
Subtotal	_____
+ Sales Tax*	_____
+ Shipping**	_____
TOTAL	_____

* For California residents only. Please add 7.75% of the Subtotal.
** Please add $4 shipping for first book and $2 for each additional book

Name: _____

Organization: _____

Address: _____

City/State/Zip: _____

Phone: _____ Email: _____

Payment Method (circle): **Check/Money Order** **Visa/Mastercard**

Card #: _____ Exp. Date: _____

Signature _____

Make checks payable to: Lawpsided Press
Mail orders to: P.O. Box 1867, Chino Hills, CA 91709
Phone orders to: (866) 222-7024
Fax orders to: (909) 393-0922
Email orders to: orders@ifitdoesnotfit.com